Philosophical Foundations
of English Socialism

Philosophical Foundations of English Socialism

ADAM B. ULAM

1 9 6 4
OCTAGON BOOKS, INC.
NEW YORK

Reprinted 1964
by special arrangement with Harvard University Press

OCTAGON BOOKS, INC.
175 FIFTH AVENUE
NEW YORK, N. Y. 10010

LIBRARY OF CONGRESS CATALOG CARD NUMBER: 64-24847

Printed in U.S.A. by
NOBLE OFFSET PRINTERS, INC.
NEW YORK 3, N. Y.

Preface

This book is neither a history of the British Labour Party nor a systematic account of its present policies. Having entered upon a study of some of the theoretical sources of English socialism I found myself compelled to comment, however briefly, on the intellectual atmosphere, policies, and dilemmas surrounding the Welfare State as conceived and built by English socialists. Political and even economic institutions are often crystallized expressions of political theories. I have attempted to illustrate this relationship in the case of a great social movement, which, descended from the political tradition of the West, seeks new answers to the problem of democracy in an industrial society.

Putting one's own opinions in print is essentially an immodest endeavor, and the author must always remain grateful to those whose help and encouragement assisted him in formulating his ideas and in persuading him that they might be of interest to others. It is pleasant to recall my debt to Professor William Yandell Elliott of Harvard for his constant advice as well as for the stimulus provided by his own writings and teaching. I have learned much from discussions with my friends, whether on subjects touching on this book or simply on politics and political theory in general. Here I would like to mention with gratitude Professors Samuel H. Beer and Louis Hartz of Harvard, Peter Bachrach of Bryn Mawr, and William H. Riker of Lawrence College.

I am indebted to the Clarendon Press for allowing me to quote from T. H. Green's *Prolegomena to Ethics;* and to Mrs. Ellen Bosanquet for similar permission in regard to Bosanquet's *The Principle of Individuality and Value.*

A. B. U.

October 1950
Cambridge, Massachusetts

Contents

Philosophical Foundations
of English Socialism

1

Introduction

There are few fields of human endeavor in which more intellectual effort has been expended and against which more charges of uselessness have been preferred than the realm of political science. Especially the attempt to theorize about politics must often appear either as fantasy or second guessing.

Against this dismissal we must count the opposite viewpoint: to political ideas — to social and economic ideas in general — have often been ascribed magic powers transcending and affecting the organic forces regulating the life of societies. The Keynesian view, "it is ideas which count," is well known. Very close to it is the view put forward by Hayek in his *Road to Serfdom:* the course of Western civilization has been fatally affected by the "false" ideas of collectivism and pseudo planning which are likely to culminate everywhere, as they already have in some countries, in dictatorship.

If the importance of ideas, and of political ideas in particular, is exaggerated by the latter writers then let us remember that they are not alone in their opinions. Every political theorist (and Keynes and Hayek deserve this appellation) must believe consciously or unconsciously in the power of ideas. Be it Marx for whom ideologies and ideas are but emanations from material conditions or Pareto whose "derivations" only conceal the real and unchangeable instincts of man, or others — they all pay a tribute to the speculative, we do not say as yet rational, nature of man. For if this nature is denied why put your ideas down in writing, and with a great deal of vehemence? Hence all of political theory is an attempt to convince or to enlighten. But does this statement in itself help us to understand and weigh the relative importance and impact of various theories?

It is curious how a knowledge of history helps and yet distorts our understanding of political ideas. For the latter are too often the means of asserting human independence against the ceaseless change and pressure of history. The willingness to be led by history is only a mock humility; no political philosopher ever abdicates the role of molding his times. This is the greater aim in which class prejudices, economic interests, the religious and aesthetic bias are all contained. Political theory is a way of self-expression. Its first and binding characteristic lies in its "internal" character, in the attempt to justify "the State's ways" to men by the writer and to strike a responsive chord in the follower. Only then comes the mass of statistics, the legal and constitutional arguments, and scientific data designed to support and develop the author's position.

If this view of the meaning of political theory is adopted our interest and research in it must be correspondingly adjusted. We still ought to seek the real meaning of a theorist, but perhaps we ought not to put an undue emphasis on the detection of logical consistencies and inconsistencies of the theory. Find the core of a man's thoughts, his relation to and influence on his times and, equally important, look for what is left of his meaning and insights in the presence of today's problems — those are the things which should preoccupy us in analyzing a political theory. And if in this process of analysis we are not able to see vividly almost as if in sculptured relief the political arguments, economic issues, and intellectual crosscurrents of the relevant period — then the most thorough knowledge of the dates and statistics of the period will not help us in understanding either the man or his times.

The objection raised to the preceding views is very immediate — a political theory never exists in a vacuum. Political theories are the outgrowths of a general system of philosophy, or they may emerge from a purely historical narrative. Economic theories, works of art, almost any realm of intellectual and imaginative endeavor will often reveal a substratum of political philosophy. There is an endless variety of religious, political, and intellectual circumstances which will evoke a conscious attempt to define and analyze the governing of men. Is it legitimate in view of all these facts to consider political theory mainly as a very personal and intuitive expression on the part of the writer and to assess its importance according to the degree to which it touches and awakens similar experiences and expressions among his fellow men? Can we discuss the theories which ignore what modern psychology has taught us about human nature? Is the problem of the validity of Marxist economics irrelevant in debating Marxism?

Philosophy is in a sense the description of a vantage point from which we want to survey what surrounds us. Political philosophy is a small but integral part of this vantage point. We may arrive at this place by different routes but once there we survey the area around us, including the road we took, from a fixed point. The first problem for a theorist is to find this vantage point and to describe it. To the measure in which we allow it to be concealed by the surroundings, be they economics or psychology, political theory as such suffers. It appears as a casual deduction from another discipline, rather than a firmly entrenched and, shameful to say, a priori assumption. Try to convince a Marxist of the unreasonability of his position basing your argument on the faultiness of Marxist economics. The effort in most cases will be fruitless for the conviction has become founded on something else and no historico-economic argument will shake it. The search for certainty, historians of political thought notwithstanding, may be more important than the search for economic security or for political stability. Economic interests, social and political considerations, all are qualifying and introductory factors yet at some stage they become subsumed in this greater search.

Surely, it will be objected, most people are not so politically or theoretically minded as to go through this painful process of analysis and ultimate synthesis. Is it necessary to accept the concept of universal human rationality in order to accord to every man a conscious or unconscious choice of his political philosophy as well as of his general philosophy? What is the concept of democracy but an attempt to make this choice a conscious one rather than to allow a complete immersion in the mores and opinions of a territorial, national, or religious (using the term in the broadest sense) community. We can be free of the rationalist bias, and yet not remain blind to the great awakening of passionate interest in politics which characterizes our times. As religion was to the medieval man so have politics become to the modern man the main avenue of expression and self-assertion.

The ramifications of the new scope of politics are obvious. The ideas which in the past appealed to a small group of aristocrats and intellectuals or to a larger group of the middle class have to be rephrased, if not changed, to move a much larger audience. There is not much point today to writing a new *Prince* or a new *Leviathan* or even a new essay *On Representative Government*. An antidemocratic writer who wants to be heard, whether in the United States or in the Soviet Union, will phrase his argument in democratic terminology.

There is another curious thing about modern political theory which requires mentioning in this connection. The very fact of writing about politics gives an elitist tinge to the writer no matter what his argument may be. Whether we "open the eyes of the masses," warn them against "dangerous innovations," or urge them to shake off the "obsolete institutions," we challenge the collective wisdom of society in a manner which is somewhat undemocratic. But beyond this inherent aristocratic bias of every political writer there are various degrees of assertion. Isn't it striking that today, in contrast with what was true one hundred years ago, it is the progressive who puts his trust in an elite, who sees the best hope for a needed reform in an enlightened public official, while it is his opponent the conservative who argues against this idea? Management training, the schools of public administration, civil servants' boards for nationalized industries; don't they all testify that the frightened liberal beats his retreat to the Platonic position, while his opponent remains supremely confident that working out of history will always produce a ruling elite, but without Plato's prerequisites and without the modern liberal's safeguards?

But what is the external form of political ideas? Where is the key to the influence which the personal experience and expression, be it of a disgruntled misanthrope or of a lover of humanity, wields over the hearts and minds of other men? Croce's statement that ideas have to be warmed by love in order to be effective is a very optimistic phrasing of the problem. It is very hard to imagine a political current without a demonology of its own. We all know that there are several levels of political thought: first the philosopher with his theory, then the polemicist or the politician with his concrete postulates in place of the dialectic and the absolutes, and finally the vulgar level of discussion in which theories and reforms evaporate and what remains is the maligned and distorted picture of the enemy. The power of a philosopher lies in that he can stir up great waves of feeling and agitation. His helplessness is due to his inability to control the farther waves of his thought. The self-assertion and the desire to mold his world, of which we spoke before, are seldom granted to a theoretician. That Rousseau and Marx should have been venerated by the respective Revolutions is hardly a consolation for the fact that their theories came to life in a misshapen form. Political philosophers may have a feeling of melancholy not unlike that of a physicist or a mathematician when they contemplate the use to which their insights and discoveries are put.

What generalizations can we make about political theories if we accept the previous discussion? To paraphrase a well-known statement: no political ideas are new, some are true, and most of them matter. The three components of the statement deserve some consideration.

To trace the genealogy of an idea is a fascinating game. We seldom have, in the case of great and influential ideas, the simple relationship of derivation. Rather, we may assume, great ideas lie dormant until the spirit of the times and the power of synthesis on the part of a great thinker bring some of them to life at a particular period. But it is a facile overgeneralization to say that a man or his theory is a product of his times. Most of the great theorists do not merely register the impact of the contemporary social and economic conditions. They look either backward or forward, and even the defenders of the status quo — that is, the articulate ones — embody in their pleas the hope and argument for a change in the political and social structure of their day. Plato and Aristotle may have realized the obsolescence of the city-state of their day, yet they phrased a proud reassertion of the system. Marx admired the accomplishments of capitalism yet he prophesied and desired its doom. Were the Swiss cantons really like Rousseau's ideal community, or did he write urged by a strong antipathy to the spirit and society of his age? Examples can be multiplied where it is neither the novelty of this or that idea, for they all contain some old refrains, nor the simple impact of the times which creates great political thought. It is, rather, the impact of the times, softened and transmuted by the eternal yearning and dissatisfaction of man which produces a new theory and new conditions of the age.

"Correctness" of a political theory consists again in the extent to which it can satisfy the aspirations of its times, and yet preserve the structure of thought on man and society which will always be relevant. It must offer some tokens of spiritual and material efficacy, but more important it must ask questions, which men in the future generations will still be passionately interested in answering. To an academician a political theory offers interest insofar as it presents new and intriguing problems, insofar as it is "original" in its conception. But to a contemporary society the interest in a theory, its "proof," lies in the degree to which it can become a channel through which the interests, passions, and pleas of the moment can be put in a concrete form and "explained." Hence a theory, as asserted before, will always become simplified if it becomes popular. The attempted universality of a political theory will become discarded or twisted. It is only by an insight into his own times that the author will gain a large following. The other nuances of his thought — his nostalgia for the past or his construction of the future — will, by comparison, become pale dreams.

It is not suggested here that this futility of the theorist in his primary, if sometimes hidden, objective of molding his own times is inevitable, and that organic forces will always overcome and absorb intellectual effusions. But in order to understand the relative importance of political ideas we must first of all see how hard it is to combine inspiration with self-consciousness, dogma with tactics, and moral strictures with propaganda. Once we realize that we should not be surprised that the very few great currents of political thought which combine these contradictory elements, and have consequently earned opprobrium for their inconsistencies, have been most successful in influencing human minds and institutions.

An appreciation of this problem would help us not only to understand why modern radicals are tempted to become Marxists, but also why the nature of the temptation is different depending on the convert's social, economic, or national background. By contrast liberalism — the middle-road view — finds itself on the defensive, largely because it has lost the capacity of inspiring the same intensity of hope and fear as its rival. To recover it liberalism must not only preserve the power of its analysis and the humanity of its postulates, it must also recoup its moral fervor. And beyond it must again become an effective direction to action rather than a plea for hesitation.

The approach to truth by a political theory can mean only that different societies at different times find in it a reflection of their own problems and feelings. But this is hardly synonymous with success. Making people reflect does not necessarily mean making them act, or especially, making them act in the given direction.

The statement that most political theories, no matter how "obsolete" or absurd they may be, have some effect, means that the relationship of man to society is never completely defined and settled, and that any powerful and articulate opinion on the subject will find adherents. We should know by now how useless it is to assail a political theory as impractical. What such statements imply is that a theory should be always a deduction from the facts of politics, and that any failure to take into account the existing realities dooms a political theory to failure. But if, as we stated, the role of a political theory is also to portray visions and promise certainties, the question of its practicability becomes almost irrelevant. It is in the second stage of political thought — in the area of political action — that the theory will become fused with the considerations of social realities. The primary impulse of generous visions and postulates may then become obscured by the appeal to fear or hate, but the original impetus will still be the main driving force. A free struggle of political theories will not bring an automatic victory to the most logically constructed theory, as the liberal of the nineteenth century fondly and complacently imagined, nor will it bring an automatic triumph to the ideas which best satisfy brutal emotions, as a disillusioned rationalist of today may imagine. The intellectual success of a political theory, which in the times of historical transition and revolution will spell a political success as well, depends on the strength and genuineness of its ultimate moral appeal and on the clarity of the target it sets out to reach.

The view set here about the meaning of political theory may be summarized as follows:

1. A political theory when it expresses a *conscious* effort to define the relation between men and government is usually opposed to the existing institution. Even a defence of the status quo will contain an argument for change and modification in the existing social and political conditions.[1]

2. The function of a political theory is not limited to the presentation of a convenient mythology. Its dynamic quality is reflected in the dynamic character of the institutions of the society it foresees. Like a work of art a political theory struggles to capture and to blend the elements of universal human experience and of universal human aspirations.

3. The primary measure of success of a political theory, achieved by so few of them, lies in the extent to which the basic premises of the theory can still control the theory-in-action. What gave strength to the democratic theory, what enabled it to give Western civilization a century of unparalleled economic and intellectual progress (which, paradoxically, assured its stability), has been its internal constitutionalism which prevented its "means" from running away from the "ends." But of late exponents of the theory have found themselves increasingly doubtful of the "practicability" of its ends. They discard the traditional "ends" and "means" connection in many cases (for example, when social prog-

---

[1] To anticipate an immediate rejoinder: even the "official" political theories, as in a dictatorship, look beyond the existing reality. Rosenberg spoke in terms implying that the Third Reich of his time has gone only part way towards the realization of his ideal. The official ideology of the Soviet Union emphasizes carefully, though of late less and less frequently, that only the second stage of Marxism has been realized and that real Communism is yet to come.

ress or insurgent nationalism are concerned), and, more important, they now plead instead of prophesying.[2]

4. The main appeal of a political theory must be personal, that is, it must seek to solve political questions as they present themselves to individuals. A theory is coldly institutional only on the surface. Inside, by implication, it must present answers to the problems that men have experienced and can understand. Hobbes' theory of absolutism, for example, could have very little meaning in these terms. Though it was supposed to move and influence a much smaller group of people than a modern theory aims to, it failed to become more than a superb intellectual fabrication. Perhaps the same is true of any purely legal theory of government. But even the most legalistic theories have a substratum of appeal based on common experience. Behind the dry formulas on sovereignty, rests the profound human urge for security and stability.

Those who believe in the great democratic liberal tradition may with some justification claim that their tradition represents a political philosophy which is not only universal but also enduring in its appeal. In the long run it can only be absorbed but not destroyed by opposing principles. This is hardly a consolation for the present defensive posture of the liberal tradition, and no excuse for not attempting to revitalize it so that the theory may once again become meaningful and moving.

Ever since the beginning of the nineteenth century all political theories have had one great target — the complete domination by man over his physical environment. To fashion man in a given mold so that nothing but rational and moral considerations will affect his behavior — this aim has been the prevailing tone of political philosophies of all times. But it is only in modern times that this aim appeared to be accomplished not by acquiescence in the physical world nor by a detachment from it, but by a conscious refashioning of the environment.

The reasons for this transition in thought are obvious: the decline of the purely religious intellectual tradition and the great

---

[2] There seems to be a kind of "Gresham's law" among political ideas, which discriminates against the theories which give up the self-assurance of success and inevitability.

progress of technology. The test of performance for a political theory for a way of life has become a pragmatic one: can it provide a more successful material environment than its rivals or, in wartime, can a society professing a democratic creed defeat its totalitarian enemies?

This emphasis on the efficiency side of politics, so pronounced among the utilitarians and the positivists and by now so firmly entrenched in our official ideology, has succeeded in distorting the great democratic theory of the state. Essentially, as pointed out above, the main appeal of a political theory is personal and its main effort is educational. If it does not ceaselessly maintain that, regardless of any accident of history, its ends are the only worthwhile ones, and its means the only legitimate means, it will fail pragmatically and educationally.

It is interesting to note that the democratic-liberal theory has of late emanated increasingly from works concerned mainly with economics, Keynes and Beveridge being the most recent examples. The notion that economic progress is only a part of the education of man and society has been advanced timorously, for an emphasis on this point is thought of as typical of a reactionary theory. The pragmatic materialism which has crept into the liberal theory, and at times has taken it over, has had more than theoretical repercussions. It has twisted our vision not only in the political but also in the economic field. The search for certainty has largely disappeared from modern political theory and its place has been taken by the economic "laws." [3]

The original impetus given to political thinking by the rediscovery of economics has been lost through the preoccupation with economics per se. The main function of a political theory, which we described as an appeal to hopes and aspirations of a society by setting up goals transcending its existing condition, has been neglected. Marxism and fascism, which is so often Marxism without the hope for a final paradise of socialism, have retained the appeal of a communal goal or have utilized the emotional appeal of political demonology. In face of the successes of its enemy the democratic theory has remained stationary. Its weakness has been

[3] For a discussion of the whole problem see A. D. Lindsay, *The Modern Democratic State.*

masked by the strength of the remaining democracies. Greater than the physical threat, though, can be the corroding doubt and uncertainty which the thinking part of a society experiences in absence of a definite aim and philosophy. It may be an exaggeration to ascribe to an intellectual production the power to fill in this void, but political theory and the belief it inspires may be the spark which keeps going a machine otherwise running on borrowed time.

THE RELEVANCE OF POLITICAL THEORY

The study of political thought cannot neglect the question of its relevance. It is the time of a great social transition which gives significance and challenge to political ideas. By themselves the latter may be ineffective; they may seldom emerge from classrooms and learned journals. But a violent rupture with the past, be it a war, a revolution, or rapidly shifting economic and technological conditions, requires a theory which serves, then, not only as a catalyzer in the process, but also as the cementing factor of the new social structure.

To put the question in more direct terms: when men feel that their old institutions are no longer adequate to the needs of the hour, when their established habits and values are undermined, they are ready to ask more basic questions about the end of men and of society, questions which they were in no mood to discuss before. Perhaps the questions are not asked or there is no time to ask them, for a simple cure or a quack remedy is promptly offered and uncritically accepted. But even then the demagogues' poison is sold labeled as theory.

The complexity of problems which our generation has to face, the legacy of two wars, the precarious balance of international affairs, all those troubles and uncertainties make our times the period of transition and crisis which, since it embraces the whole world, is unparalleled in its scale if not in its intensity. The problem facing the democracies is especially acute, since they cannot accept a cure which promises to be brief and drastic, but have to look for a solution which would fit in with the tradition of the democratic society and spell out those values which still remain a figure of speech.

Can political theory define the type of society we desire and indicate some of the routes toward its achievement? Perhaps that task cannot be accomplished by politics alone. Today the scope of political life is large and bewildering. We can no longer preserve, if we ever could, the lines of separation between economics, sociology, and politics. And in taking a synthetic view of the state, we must remember to relate it to the world as a whole. There is a group of problems political theory has to tackle, some of them of a limited, others of a wider character; none of them can be studied effectively if only the problem of a nation state is kept in mind. Once again in order to be relevant a political theory needs a certain breadth of universality and an awareness of overall problems.

It also needs something else. Periods of crisis generate a general critique of the existing social order. We want to preserve certain things in our society, and we want to get rid of some institutions and features of it. Why and how? To answer "why" is to formulate the purpose of your society. To answer "how" is to attempt to find an effective political technique of transmuting your values into political and social facts.

It is noteworthy how few political theorists have attempted to combine in their philosophy those two aspects of social theory. Their search for values usually stopped at some single item: security for Hobbes, national unity for Machiavelli, protection of property rights (in the broad sense of the phrase) for Locke. This is but a testimony to the fact that a book on political theory is usually a *livre de circonstance*. Even an indictment of the existing system and a powerful plea for reform like Rousseau's *Social Contract* fails on the score of evolving a political technique. Rousseau fails to answer the question how his state is to emerge from the theory; how, lacking a divine "legislator," the General Will is to find an expression in actual institutions.

Those who, as has been the fashion of late, propose to formulate scientific politics, shelve the whole issue of values and devote their attention to what is assumed to be an objective description of political processes and techniques. When Pareto writes about politics and society, the assumption is that he is describing facts and does not consider their desirability any more than a mathematician proposes to find out whether it would be desirable for two and two to make five or six.[4] Yet this approach very often degenerates into a prescription how to "handle" people. Instead of rationally conceived values we get then myths; normal functions of citizenship give way to torchlight parades; other paraphernalia of democracy are, also, doing service for an elite or a dictator.

Social psychologists (if this title can be an exclusive property of one school) do not neglect the problem of value in their prescriptions for an ailing society. But this value emerges, curiously, from the method itself; it steals into the "scientific" part of discussion. For the utilitarians who are among the precursors of the school, social values are but the crystallizations of desirable social techniques. Bentham finds a childish delight in devising institutions and laws, which of themselves are to maximize desirable habits. Even John Stuart Mill, more mature and realistic than his great predecessor, retains an approach toward social problems which is largely mechanistic in its nature.

Two examples can be adduced which demonstrate a successful combination of the two main elements of political theory, value and technique. Paradoxically, they are found in two quite opposite camps.

Socialism as formulated by Marx and Engels and developed both by the communist and the noncommunist tradition has a definite analysis of the working of society, and also a clear idea of what the movement is after in terms of social reconstruction. To be sure, the socialist critique of capitalism is much superior to their own idea of what the socialist society is to be like.[5]

---

[4] The assumption is, to digress for a second, false. There is hardly a political theorist whose discussion bears so unmistakably traces of a definite political and social bias as Pareto.

[5] This criticism by a non-Marxist socialist, while unfair from the theoretical point of view, illustrates the practical dilemma of non-revolutionary Marxism: "Not only are the Neo-Marxians without any social theory in the sense that they have never applied themselves to the task of elaborating the principles upon which a democratic and communal society must rest, but they appear to be unaware that one is necessary. All they see is that power today is in the hands of capitalists, and they want to see it transferred into those of the workers. That is very good so far as it goes. But it is insufficient for the purpose of reconstructing society, which they would be called upon to do if ever they succeeded to power; because if industry suddenly changed hands and the salariat were banished, as they propose, everything would not go on sweetly as before. The centre of gravity of industry would have completely changed . . . It is vain to suppose that without clearly defined

The group of people responsible for the Constitution of the
United States was another body of political theorists and practical
politicians who managed to combine the mechanical, the institutional aspect of politics with a clear concept of the purpose of
society. Genuine constitutionalism is primarily the recognition of
ethical principles which should govern men in society. The writers
of the Constitution and of the related documents showed an amazing appreciation of social and economic realities underlying political theories. The whole series of documents starting with the
Declaration of Independence and ending with the Federalist pa-
pers show this nexus between idealism and pragmatism. There are,
one might say, three layers of thought in the whole series. The
first is the ethical end of man and society. The second is the consequent formulation of the long-range interest of society: representative government, a continuation and definition of the current
concept of liberty. Finally, we see an actual appraisal of the balance of forces within America of the day, an appraisal not done
with an unbiased eye, and a consequent network of laws and institutions.

The two examples given above, oversimplified as they are,
illuminate the task of modern political thought which addresses
itself to the idea of the democratic state. Principally, it is the search
for an ethical end and for the policies to implement it. Our effort
will be to find out whether such a synthesis is possible, and if so
what are its main ingredients. Such a reconstruction is attempted
here not in terms of a genealogy of ideas, but in terms of specula-
tion as to what the ideas to be discussed really meant and of what
service they can be to us today.

No apologies are offered for using English political thought as
a fulcrum for the discussion. British political institutions and the
thought applied to them constitute one of the most important
battlegrounds for the future of democratic government. To take
the current of thought which tries to redefine and formulate the
concrete idea of democracy involves the danger of ignoring the

principles to guide them men unaccustomed to power would prove equal to the
task. They would be like amateurs in possession of a powerful and unfamiliar
weapon which, mishandled, would be much more likely to destroy them than the
enemy." Arthur J. Penty, *Guilds and the Social Evils* (London: Allen and Unwin,
1919), p. 100.

antagonistic strain which finds its precursors in the thought of people like Bacon, Hobbes, Carlyle, and others. But present in the democratic tradition is a constant debate with its critics, as well as a constant process of readjustment to changing social and economic conditions. A discussion of idealism, socialism, or pluralism must involve the study not only of the formulation of those ideas, but also of some of the basic problems of the modern state.

2

Idealism

Idealism as a philosophy and as a political theory answers to many definitions. Political idealism, with which we deal here, can be characterized in a most rudimentary way as the insistence that the state is not a mechanical contrivance or a utilitarian device, but a projection of man's moral self, a necessary means and implementation of his full development. To put the problem this way is to see immediately the genealogy of idealism: the strain which runs through Plato, Rousseau, and Hegel. And also to see its significance today: isn't the modern state, whether democratic or nondemocratic, assuming functions and powers which would indicate, consciously or unconsciously, an acceptance of this basic premise of idealism?

This study deals with the idealistic position as defined originally by Thomas Hill Green, Bernard Bosanquet, and Francis Herbert Bradley. Before speaking of its content and contribution it is well to realize the general tone of the school.

It is a peculiar characteristic of modern political thought that it has emerged so often from academic circles. In this case we have the phenomenon of three Victorian thinkers, products of the unique academic atmosphere of Oxford of the second half of the nineteenth century, who evolved a political philosophy antithetic in its approach and conclusions to the English society which surrounded them. Their politics emerges from their general philosophy. The mechanics of politics, political parties, actual institutions of government — they are all neglected in the writings of Green and Bosanquet. What the writings do exhibit is a strong influence of Platonic tradition, an influx of the German idealism of Kant and Hegel, and, in the case of Green, a definitely religious tone of political thinking.

The type of classical education received by the English upper and middle classes of that generation had a peculiar intellectual and social effect. In the midst of a modern industrial society, young men were led to admire the thinking ability and discipline of the Greeks and their pursuit of knowledge for its own sake out of a craving for beauty and order. Pragmatism and utilitarianism alike were held at disadvantage when compared to the Greek ideal of pure intellectual curiosity[1] and a type of moral absolutism.

The intellectual atmosphere could not but engender a certain affinity with the ideas of the man who symbolizes Greek culture at its highest. Some of Plato's moral absolutism, his extreme rationalism, his idea — spotlighted in *The Symposium* — of human personality finding its fullest development in creativeness — all those elements characterize the tone of English idealism. Both by example and by implication the Greek idea of the interrelationship of the individual and the state found converts.[2]

And yet the Greco-Roman world of ideas and literature was only a part of the matrix from which grew the political philosophy of English idealism. For all its genius and charm the Greek heritage offered little to a political philosopher of the nineteenth cen-

[1] "If Western civilization had followed the view of Professor Dewey and the pragmatists and regarded knowledge and thought as mere means to the solution of practical problems, we should have been today as lacking in science as are the civilizations of India and China." W. T. Stace, *The Destiny of Western Man,* p. 103.

[2] One who was almost of the same generation and whose early interest was wholly in science was to testify to the pervading effect of the classical education: "Altogether we were a happy set of boys, receiving a deplorably narrow education to fit us for the modern world. But I will disclose one private conviction based upon no confusing research, that, as a training in political imagination, the Harvard School of Politics and Government cannot hold a candle to the old fashioned English classical education of half a century ago." A. N. Whitehead, *Essays in Science and Philosophy,* p. 39.

tury. Its view of good life, of an ideal society, tended to be, when put in concrete terms of political theory, cold and formalistic. For all the intensity of feeling and the notions of brotherhood exhibited in their drama and poetry, the Greeks were too much hampered by their institutions and the parochialism of their national life to be sympathetic to democracy or to the idea of cosmopolitan society. In contemplating the fate and influence on history, both of the utopias they sketched and of the "best practical" states they painted, one is again reminded of Croce's saying that ideas have to be warmed by love to be really effective.

It is a strong infusion of Christian ethics which provides the second element of the tone of idealist philosophy. The religious tone of much of the idealists' writings makes them somewhat hard to digest for a modern student of politics, but there is no doubt that to them it was this feeling which lay at the basis of all social reform and personal satisfaction. It may sound a bit priggish (as all of political philosophy does in a sense), but at the bottom of our "values" lies the perception of "good life" involving the full development of mental and emotional faculties of man. Morality is a process of realization.[3] It is in a sense a ceaseless effort at improvement and inquiry. Life, idealism holds, has no mercy for a society or a man who slackens in this effort at self-improvement. For all its academic character the movement has a certain vigor of thought and distrust of excessive intellectualism.[4]

The discussion illustrates another characteristic of the idealist school. Society and the individual are taken at one and the same level of argument. We do not find here the dichotomy of values which characterizes a "realist" theory of politics à la Hobbes. The state and the individual are to be judged by the same yardstick: their share and progress in the realization of that aesthetic combination of intellect and emotion which represents the quintessence of Western civilization. The effort signals abandonment of the notion that the state is an artificial creation. But farther than

[3] Bradley, *Ethical Studies*, p. 234.
[4] "This or that human being, this or that passing stage of culture may remain in this region of weariness, of false self-approval and self-contempt, but for the race as a whole this is impossible . . . It has never done it, and while man is man, it certainly never will do it." Bradley, p. 315.

that it forecasts a rethinking of the state's function, which is of deepest significance.[5]

Among the three philosophers we are considering, Green recognizes most clearly that the same yardstick must be applied to the actions of the state that we use in judging the performance of an individual. He is thoroughly imbued with the spirit of Kantian philosophy. Bradley and Bosanquet wander dangerously near to the Hegelian conclusion that the state is the higher self of the individual, and somehow not to be judged by the criteria of private morality.[6]

Yet the general spirit of the philosophy is characterized by the search for a formula to define the moral task of the state, and to set a single standard of value which would guide men in their public and private actions. The ideal is not to be the austere and unapproachable "duty for duty's sake," or an attempt to grasp physical satisfaction (in a broad sense of the word), or still more absurd to measure it, but the effort at "self-realizedness," as put somewhat awkwardly by Bradley.[7]

The tone of emotional intensity and unceasing intellectual inquiry found in idealistic philosophy is typified in Green's words: "on the other hand, just because it is self-satisfaction that is sought in all willing in self-realizing subject, it is only in the attainment of its own perfection that such satisfaction can be found, the object of will is intrinsically or potentially, and tends to become actually the same as that of reason. We must suppose that this confidence implies a great deal of discipline. It is a discipline though, not of denial or suppression, but resting on the conviction that the natural impulses have to be fused with those higher in-

[5] "The fact is that the decisive issue is not whether we call the individual or society the 'end' but what we take to be the nature at once of individuals and society." Bosanquet, *The Philosophical Theory of the State*, p. 81.

[6] Compare Green's statement on war — "And this is to say that the source of war between states lies in their incomplete fulfilment of their function in the fact that there is some defect in the maintenance or reconciliation of rights among their subjects" — with Bosanquet's assertion that parallels from private morality cannot be applied to such state actions as war (*Lectures on the Principles of Political Obligation*, London, 1895, p. 172, and *The Philosophical Theory of the State*, p. 328).

[7] Bradley, p. 261.

terests which aim at a higher, more enduring pleasure and hence
human perfection." [8]

We begin to perceive the tone of idealist philosophy and the
values it seeks. It seeks an earnest approach to those issues of
politics and morals which, though preached about so often that
they have become truisms, remained divorced from the actuality
of political life. First of all, Green seeks the spirit of constant inquiry and scrutiny by the whole society as to the way both political life and individual conduct should be pursued. He is building
through his philosophy, without any concrete examples, the most
radical utopia of them all, a society always intellectually alive in
which every individual discusses in Platonic manner the basic
issues of politics; in which every individual seeks an understanding of Christian ethics. A philosophy of this kind must always
remain at an "impractical" level — it can inseminate others with
ideas; of itself it is too far removed from everyday reality to be
of direct influence.

The same tone steals into the discussion, or the first approaches
to discussion, of political matters. "Will not force is the basis of
the state" says Green in one of his most characteristic statements.
Again, it is an ethical precept rather than a statement of historical
fact. For an individual, idealism holds, strong will is a prerequisite
to personal happiness, to moral virtue. [9] Hence freedom must mean
more than the freedom to be influenced by our environment. Such
freedom is little more than the freedom of a rat in a maze. Man
craves a more direct authority over his life. "An action which expresses character has no must in the physical sense about it." [10]
Man is endowed with a sense of dignity and independence, surely
a necessary prerequisite for his function as a citizen, and by a clear
conception of what he is and what he wants. [11] Society should help

---

[8] Green, *Lectures on the Principles of Political Obligation,* p. 21.

[9] "Strong will" according to Green ". . . means that it is the man's habit to
set clearly before himself certain objects in which he seeks self-satisfaction and that
he does not allow himself to be drawn aside from these by suggestions of chance
desires." *Prologomena to Ethics,* p. 118.

[10] *Ibid.,* p. 120.

[11] Compare "Nothing whatever besides yourself determines either casually or
otherwise just what constitutes your individuality . . . And here and now your
individuality in your act *is* your freedom." Royce, *The World and the Individual,*
p. 489.

him to arrive at that conception, but the act of willing the striving for self-realization must be his. Here we have the seed of the idea of democracy giving the individual a wide range of opportunities for the realization of his capacities and desires, and providing an atmosphere conducive to his moral growth. The concept of moral freedom may be out of fashion with the social psychologist of today, but the argument for it when taken in conjunction with the role of the state it envisages is far from being just rhetoric. It sees that under suitable social conditions man can realize the ideal and, once arrived, his standards will withstand the adversity of external forces through the vision of a higher good.[12]

It is the awareness that the individual is the starting and final point of the moral process which provides a sharp breaking point between English idealism and its German counterpart. Hegel, if any generalization is permissible about his philosophy, found the state at the end of the road. The state was for him the "higher self," not only in the sense of helping the individual along to realize his moral self, but also as an embodiment of reason and morality, separate from the individual yet expressing, though he might not know it, his higher instincts. For Green, if not for Bosanquet, the state is only a means, a supremely important means, but meaningful only insofar as it helps the individual to realize his higher needs, not scorning the more prosaic ones. Hence, practical results of both philosophies diverge widely.[13]

Green illustrates the blending of German idealism and of a religious strain in a passage remarkable for its idealistic rephrasing of Bentham's democratic principle:

Thus in a conscientious citizen of a modern Christendom reason without, reason within, reason as objective and reason as subjective, reason as the better spirit of the social order in which he lives, and reason as

---

[12] "So long as a man presents himself as possibly existing in some better state than that in which he actually is, and that he does so is implied even in his denial that the possibility can be realized — there is something in him to respond to whatever moralizing influences society in any of its forms or institutions, themselves the gradual outcome through ages of man's free effort to better himself, may bring to bear on him." Green, *Prologomena to Ethics*, p. 126.

[13] John Dewey put it succinctly if somewhat unfairly in speaking of Hegel and his school: ". . . persons who profess no regard for happiness as a test of action have an unfortunate way of living up to their principle by making others unhappy." *German Philosophy and Politics*, p. 91.

his loyal recognition and interpretation of that spirit — these being but different aspects of one and the same reality, which is the operation of the divine mind in man — combine judgment and obedience to the judgment which we variously express by saying that every human person has an absolute value; that humanity in the person of every one is always to be treated as an end, never merely as a means; that in the estimate of that well-being which forms the true good every one is to count for one, and no one for more than one; that every one has a "suum" which every one else is bound to render him.[14]

The tone of idealism is, therefore, not that of a philosophy which preaches that mankind can be improved by lifting ourselves by our bootstraps. There are seeds in it of a vigorous democratic feeling, and a plea for a stronger role for the state. A moral individual and a healthy society requires a modicum of material prerequisites. Green and Bosanquet wrote when the utilitarian and positivist philosophies were in ascendance; when it seemed that the progress in prosperity and technology will of itself bring all the needed blessings to the world. Yet they saw that the material progress was in itself not enough and that a clearer formulation of democracy, and of the relationship of the individual to the state, was a prerequisite to a new theory of the democratic state. This task in itself requires a certain vigor and completeness. Too many philosophers of the age, as well as of our own, generalize their own social and political views or expand an intellectual "ennui," into a pessimistic or fatalistic philosophy of human nature. Idealism while lacking in concreteness has a sense of balance and completeness:

When a man sits down in a calm hour to consider what his permanent well-being consists in, what it is that in desiring he really desires, it is not indeed to be supposed that he traces the desire back to its ultimate sources in his self-objectifying personality, or that he thinks of its object in the abstract form of that which will satisfy the demand arising from such a personality. But if unbiased either by particular passions or by philosophical prepossessions, he will identify his well-being with an order of life which that demand has brought into existence. The thought of his well-being will be to him the thought of himself as living

[14] *Prologomena to Ethics* (Oxford: Clarendon Press, 1929), p. 253.

in the successful pursuit of various interests which the order of society
— taking the term in the widest sense — has determined for him; interests ranging perhaps from provision for his family to the improvement
of the public health or to the production of a system of philosophy.[15]

The passage quoted sets the individual in a more modest
position than that assigned to him by the utilitarian school of
liberalism. The "order of society" appears as a determinant influence on the individual's life. If that statement were coupled with
an assertion that the order cannot be changed but must be let
alone, then we would not err in classifying Green as a conservative. However, he does nothing of the sort, he presents his view
to develop the thesis that society is of such a tremendous importance that its foundations have to be overhauled and improved to
allow moral existence on the part of its members. Society for him
has no meaning unless it maintains and develops moral individuality of its members and unless they are conscious of it.[16]

Of Green, Caird wrote with a great deal of justification: "If
there was a third quality by which he was distinguished it was

---

[15] Green, *Prologomena to Ethics*, p. 275.

[16] Bosanquet diverges from Green towards the Hegelian view: "But granted
that nothing has value which is not in some sort a personal consciousness, the question is not settled how much more than its given self at any moment such a consciousness may imply as the unit of value to which it belongs. The first, we might
well argue as in effect we argued above, when we said that in a personal consciousness we accepted a standard that goes beyond the state of consciousness of a
conscious being. By a person, or a being partaking in individuality (even if we
include in our idea animals and young children), we presumably mean some sort of
a whole; and the states of consciousness are not wholes. But further, the real question is whether two or more so-called persons can be members of the same whole or
unity for purposes of valuation. Are they to be valued as given, or do they, by form-
ing an integral part of greater wholes, acquire a value completely other than that
which they would prima facie possess? I hold it at this point as was indicated
above, a concession of enormous importance, that the value of any state of consciousness is said not necessarily to be known to its subject or to any actual judge.
This seems to remove all compulsion to interpret the value as an immediate aspect
of a given complex. It is consistent with the view that the significance and implications of the complex, however latent and remote to the ordinary spectator, are
the grounds of its value." *The Principle of Individuality and Value* (London: Macmillan, 1912), p. 312. The same, dangerous from the liberal point of view, concession is seen in Bosanquet's statement: "The doctrine which we have been opposing
is probably a reaction against the exaggerated claims of social good to be the only
good, but it seems a mistake to push it so far as to deny that the State is a name
for a special form of self-transcendence, in which individuality strongly anticipates
the character of its perfection." *Ibid.*, p. 316.

by an intensely democratic or Christian tone of feeling that could
not tolerate the thought of privilege and constantly desired for
every class and individual a full share in all the great heritage of
humanity." [17] It is questionable whether the "Christian or democratic tone of feeling" can constitute in itself a political philosophy, but it is certainly an important part of it. This feeling is an
antidote to the notion that material progress is the only way to
humanity's improvement and salvation, or as Mr. Laski wrote —
a strange sentiment in a socialist — "We must begin with the
assumption that the sole method open to mankind by which he
can improve his lot is an increasing mastery of nature." [18] Idealist
philosophy, on the contrary, has to assume that a certain modicum
of material well-being must be a prerequisite of a society and of
an individual, but also that material progress by itself is neutral.
A concrete sense of development and purpose comes from the
realization of those ideals, which indeed require favorable material conditions as the soil, but which grow out of it, and ought to
acquire qualities undetermined by economic conditions of social
life.[19]

The implications of this most general statement of idealism
would lead to two conclusions. First, idealism is an ethical creed.
It preaches continuous striving by the individual at self-improvement, at translating into action those moral precepts, about which
the civilized world has grown so blasé. In the second place it
would flow logically from its tone that idealism should advocate
a concept of the state which would make it a serviceable instrument of social and economic reform. We shall see later on whether

[17] Preface to the fifth edition of Green's *Prologomena to Ethics.*

[18] *Faith, Reason and Civilization,* p. 32.

[19] The notion of mind growing out of primitive conditions of life and then
fashioning the material conditions to suit the purpose of life is not alien to one of
the most severe critics of idealism: "The primitive intelligence is useful to the
organism as a more elastic method of adjusting itself to its environment. As the
mental powers develop, the tables are turned, and the mind adjusts its environment
to its own needs. 'Mihi res non me rebus subjungere conor' is the motto that it
takes for its own. With the mastery of external nature applied science has made
us all familiar. But the last enemy that man shall overcome is himself. The internal
conditions of life, the physiological basis of mental activity, the sociological laws
that operate for the most part unconsciously, are parts of the 'environment' which
the self-conscious intelligence has to master and it is on this mastery that the
'regnum hominun' will rest." L. T. Hobhouse, *Mind in Evolution,* p. 443.

the latter implication is actually justified. But it should be obvious that the two ideas go hand in hand, and that it is indeed a lame political theory which concentrates solely either on moral preaching or on advocating social and economic reform.

We should expect an idealist philosopher who, like Green, advocates democracy to develop a more integral concept of democratic society than the one sketched by a utilitarian. For the latter democracy was for most part the means to achieve certain ends he desired. Nothing is more characteristic in this respect than the evolution of political views of Bentham who traveled from the admiration of an enlightened despot through a belief in aristocracy to the final espousal of democracy. Once the newest device did not provide the desired result the road could be traversed backwards. Here one thinks of Pareto, as one of many modern economists and political thinkers, who finding democracy or rather parliamentarianism not to his liking abandoned liberalism of his early days to struggle towards an elitist theory and to end in fascism. Idealism on the other hand has to seek democracy as one of its ends and not as a mere means of economic or social reform. It does not cling to a few items of value realized by nineteenth-century Western society, but seeks a more comprehensive view of the end of man and of society.

Does the conception of values as envisaged by idealism imply an actual religious faith? Idealism does not rest on any formal religion, though it has, as observed before, a great deal of religious spirit about it. "The will to be perfect need not be apprehended as non-temporal, only as a finite realization which is above or superior to this or that finite." [20] Bradley, the most religious and Neo-Platonic in his tone among the three thinkers even in his most ecstatic passages, does not formulate a plea for an actual religious system:

Be it as may the hunt after pleasure in any shape has proved itself a delusion . . . and the finite realization of my station was truth indeed, and a happiness that called us to stay, but was too narrow to satisfy wholly the spirit's hunger . . . Here our morality is consummated in oneness with God, and everywhere we find that immortal Love, which

[20] Green, *Lectures on the Principles of Political Obligation*, p. 204.

builds itself forever on contradiction, but in which the contradiction is eternally resolved.[21]

The passage illustrates some of the tone of idealist philosophy. If a political philosophy has to be understood and be a social force as well it cannot afford to remain in the realm of vagueness and near-mysticism. It is characteristic of idealism, and it has contributed to so much misunderstanding of its message, that it sometimes exhibits a quality of tone which is uncharitably described as priggishness. But this fact cannot obscure its value nor should it deter us from a most serious study of the movement. In terms of its influence and in terms of the possibilities it offers for a formulation of democracy, idealism ranks very high. It does not skip the most fundamental question of value. It attempts to put this question without dogmatism, and yet it avoids the air of eclecticism and scepticism that cannot but be harmful to a political theory which attempts to set in motion a social movement. Perhaps it is the function of the political philosopher to set a series of fundamental and relevant questions against which the problems of today are to be discussed. Idealism creates such a background, and the discussion of its actual content will show that in addition to its tone it contributes some of the seminal ideas of the modern search for democracy.

THOMAS HILL GREEN

The facts of a philosopher's life are of a secondary importance insofar as the appraisal of his work is concerned. He has, after all, the claim to be judged mainly by his work: on the basis of its accuracy, relevance, and insight. Yet while the personality of a writer is of secondary interest to a commentator, the sources of his ideas, the intellectual atmosphere which he breathed are not. They provide a setting for his ideas, they explain his intellectual growth,

[21] Bradley, *Ethical Studies,* p. 342. Compare: "But what if man had eyes to see the true beauty — the divine beauty, I mean, pure and clear and unalloyed, not clogged with the pollutions of mortality and all the colours and vanities of human life — Thither looking, and holding converse with the true beauty, simple and divine? Remember how in that communion only beholding beauty with the eye of mind, he will be enabled to bring forth, not images of beauty but realities (for he has hold not of an image but of a reality) and bringing forth and nourishing true virtue to become the friend of God and be immortal if mortal man may." *Symposium,* Jowett, ed., I. 582.

and serve as a useful clue as to what he may have been trying to say.

Thomas Hill Green was born in 1836 and died in 1882. His active life thus encompassed the middle Victorian period. No other period in modern history has probably contained a conviction similar to that of the Victorian belief that civilized man knew where he was going, and that the future course of history would merely develop and enlarge the ideas and institution of the present. From such complacent thoughts Green may have been partially saved by the peculiar and ever-present conditions of academic life which breed unrest and spiritual dissatisfaction among its votaries.

His was a typically academic background and career. He went through Rugby and in 1855 entered Balliol College. It was with Balliol and Oxford that his life was to be connected from then on until his death. His tutor had been Benjamin Jowett, who became Master of Balliol in 1870, and who was to make the college a connecting link between the worlds of politics and intellect of England. Green's own life did not present any outward signs of brilliant academic success. Long a fellow of Balliol he was elected four years before his death to the Whyte professorship of moral philosophy. It was as a professor of moral philosophy that he delivered the lectures later published as *The Principles of Political Obligation,* which constitute his only systematic treatment of political philosophy.

Green's public activity paralleled his political ideas. Though his actual participation in political life extended only to municipal politics and his other active interests were mainly in the field of educational reforms and temperance he spoke clearly and definitely on the most important political issues of his day. A part of Green's political make-up was his devotion to what was to become known as "Gladstonian liberalism": a strong dislike of adventurous foreign policy; the idea of reconciliation and reform in Ireland; some doubts as to whether the Church of England should continue in its position as the established church.

On the other hand his ideas on social and economic questions of the day went beyond those of the old-fashioned liberalism. He was, as English political terminology of those times went, a radical with strong ideas about the duty of the state to interfere with individual freedom wherever social needs warranted it. We shall explore that ambiguous statement later on. Here it is worthwhile to observe that Green's political philosophy is, especially on the subject of social and economic reform, similar to that of John Stuart Mill's last stage of thought. Green said what Mill would have said earlier in his life and more fully had he not been burdened with the incubus of early utilitarianism. If we look for a social philosophy which would be most antithetic to that of Green in its spirit and conclusions, we shall find it in the works of Herbert Spencer. Green symbolizes in a sense the final development of English liberalism; John Locke would have recognized his philosophy and not wholly disapproved of it. Herbert Spencer carries the same seed to a quite different fruition. The two of them offer definite yet irreconcilably different definitions of the basic interest of liberalism: freedom and individualism.

If Green symbolizes in a sense the end of one line of liberal tradition and its transition to a quite different line of reasoning then his philosophy must exhibit certain struggle and inconsistency. It is only a mediocre political philosopher who due to lack of imagination and intellectual ferment is completely and cheerfully consistent. What are these two elements struggling in his thought?

The first principle is his preoccupation with freedom and his attempt at a definition of the concept. Green spells out the dilemma in his lectures, *Liberal Legislation and Freedom of Contract:*

When we speak of freedom as something to be so highly prized, we mean a positive power or capacity of doing or enjoying, and that, too, something that we do or enjoy in common with others. We mean by it a power which each man exercises through the help or security given to him by his fellow-men and which he in turn helps to secure for them. When we measure the progress of a society by its growth in freedom, we measure it by the increasing development and exercise on the whole of those powers of contributing to social good with which we believe the members of the society to be endowed; in short, by the greater power on the part of the citizens as a body to make the most and best of themselves. Thus, though of course there can be no freedom among men who act not willingly but under compulsion, yet on the other hand the mere removal of compulsion, the mere enabling a man to do as he likes, is in itself no contribution to true freedom.[22]

Here Green hints towards a theory of "positive freedom" which is his main preoccupation, as we shall see, and which leads him to postulate reforms quite congenial to a modern liberal. But there is in Green's writings a trace of a rather dangerous postulation of the "positive freedom," somewhat akin to the "real freedom" of antidemocratic variety. It comes out in his essay, "The English Commonwealth," in which he observes:

The higher enthusiasm which breathed in Cromwell and Vane, was not puritanic or English merely. It belonged to the universal spiritual force which as ecstasy, mysticism, quietism, philosophy, is in permanent collision with the carnal interests of the world, and which, if it conquers them for a moment, yet again sinks under them, that it may transmute them thoroughly to its service.

And quoting the words of Vane about the people of England being asleep, Green adds:

They have slept, we may say, another two hundred years. If they should yet wake and be hungry, they will find their food in the ideas which with much blindness and weakness, he vainly offered them, cleared and ripened by a philosophy of which he did not dream.[23]

The philosophy to which Green refers at the end of the passage is clearly that of Hegel. The whole passage and the essay itself are pervaded by a rather uncritical admiration for the Commonwealth — for Cromwell and Vane in particular. What Green shows is enthusiasm for revolution whenever it liberates the spiritual energies of the people, no matter what its form or consequences may be. The English Revolution is for him "the enterprise of projecting into sudden reality the impulse of spiritual freedom." [24] Thus there is a conflict in him between the liberal anxious to establish a philosophical basis for much needed reforms and to work for them gradually, and the somewhat adventurous and impatient philosopher of history driven to admire great historical cataclysms for their sheer power and magnitude as well as for the great concepts they embodied.

[22] Green, *Works* (London: Longmans, Green, 1900), vol. III.
[23] *Ibid.*, p. 364.
[24] *Ibid.*, p. 363.

The latter position is not the prevailing one with Green. He wrote with a fine insight and in the rationalist tradition that "It is the true nemesis of human life that any spiritual impulse, not accompanied by clear comprehensive thought, is enslaved by its own realization." [25] His enthusiasm for a social upheaval even when accompanied by supression, as long as it frees the people's spiritual energies, never oversteps its bounds. It remains merely a historical perspective; he would not use the same standard of judgment in connection with contemporary society. But even as a historical analysis Green's viewpoint reveals a certain gap in his understanding of the process of politics, which is perhaps characteristic of idealism as a whole. The process of politics is thought of too exclusively as a movement of ideas and of the waves of spiritual excitement which project the ideas into reality. That there is an institutional and social context of political changes idealism is aware, but never elaborates the theme too closely. When it comes to social reform Green considers the issue as a moral obligation to remedy individual injustices, but he forgets that social conditions are in themselves a product and a factor of politics, and that to arouse moral indignation is but the first step in the process of reform. But perhaps we should not criticize idealism from the point of view of economic determinism.

Green's political ideas are enunciated systematically in his *Lectures on the Principles of Political Obligation*. The volume embodies his study on "the different senses of Freedom," and the lectures delivered at Oxford in his capacity as Professor of Moral Philosophy. They deal with the views of several thinkers on the subject: Spinoza, Hobbes, Rousseau, Locke, and Austin. Also we have a discussion of the "rights" of the state over the individual in several spheres: those of property, morality, war, and so forth. The analysis is a philosophical one: the writers discussed are torn out of their historical contexts, and their theories evaluated on largely ethical grounds. Green's own definitions of the problems fall into the same category. This is no treatise on actual politics; an attempt is made to evaluate various political problems rather abstractly and to give them a universal appearance.

The problems with which Green struggles have already been

[25] *Ibid.*, p. 332.

adumbrated. They are essentially contained in three questions: what is the individual, what is the state in relation to the individual, and what can the state do for the individual. Rather than being a study of "political obligations," which would give it a legalistic flavor which it certainly has not, Green's work is a study in mutual and moral duties of man and society centered around the phenomenon of the state.

The question of terminology has more than a technical interest. It was, in general, difficult for a British thinker of Green's generation to conceive a clear definition of the state. The main preoccupation of British liberals until John Stuart Mill had been to delimit the province of the state in favor of individual freedom. The tacit assumption had always been that "the state" is really the government of the moment and as such it is not to be trusted with more than necessary powers.

Hegel formulated the idealist definition of the state and put it upon a higher level than his "society" which was simply a network of social institutions. Green took over the idealist concept of the state, but not with Hegel's completeness. The state is for him a projection of man's moral self, but he cannot entirely liberate himself from the tradition that the actual state is also a government which may fail to live up to the ideal. Hence Green is preoccupied with minority rights and the rights of the individual against the state, issues which are ignored by Rousseau and Hegel.

Green's use of the term *society* also requires explaining. Again, he is placed between two distinct traditions. In the Lockian tradition there was very little place left for what the modern concept of society implies. Instead one had the concept of the autonomous individual linked with his fellow citizens by the artificial bonds of the state. On the other hand, Hegel envisaged the "civil community" or society as a network of classes, social institutions, and what we would call today the routine and uncontroversial function of the state like charity, preservation of order, and so forth. To Hegel this "civil society" was definitely inferior to the state as the latter "has a totally different relation to the individual. It is the objective spirit and he [citizen] has his truth, real existence and ethical status only in being a member of it." [26] Rousseau,

[26] Hegel, *Philosophy of Right*, p. 240.

whom Hegel credits with discovering but also with misunderstanding the "state will," thought of the state — the General Will — as rescuing man from society and liberating his moral self.

Green's position, as we shall see, relies somewhat on Hegel's and Rousseau's concept of society. Yet in a sense his views on the subject are distinct. Society is for him the complex of social institutions of various kinds like family, property, and so forth. They all have a common purpose: the fullest development of the individual as a moral being in the sense which we shall explore later on. The state is the most conscious and purposeful organ of society, and as such it should readjust social institutions for the common purpose. Unlike Rousseau and Hegel, Green does not abandon individualism. Unlike that of the utilitarians, his individualism does not lead him to overlook society and to minimize the role of the state.

Man is assumed by Green to be a moral being, that is, the individual always seeks moral self-improvement. This is an a priori assumption which underlies idealist philosophy and any failure to tolerate it makes the discussion fruitless. Green himself makes no elaborate investigation of his assumptions. He is content to describe his position as being diametrically opposed to that of utilitarianism, which according to him "recognizes no vocation of man but the attainment of pleasure and avoidance of pain." [27] The vocation of man according to Green is the attainment of goodness, the necessary condition of which is individual freedom. What do these two terms mean?

What Green implies by the term "goodness" has a strong undertone of altruism. It is, first, the ability to conceive a disinterested ideal. [28] Furthermore, the individual should conceive the ideal not merely as a personal one, but should be willing to grant the capacity for its satisfaction to all the members of the society. [29]

[27] *Lectures on the Principles of Political Obligation,* p. 43.

[28] "The highest moral goodness we found was an attribute of character, in so far as it issued in acts done for the sake of their goodness, not for the sake of any pleasure or any satisfaction of desire which they bring to the agent." *Ibid.,* p. 29.

[29] "Hence on the part of every person ("person" in the moral sense explained) the claim, more or less articulate and reflected on, to rights on his own part is co-ordinate with his recognition on the part of others. The capacity to conceive a common good as one's own, and to regulate the exercise of one's powers by reference to a good which others recognize, carries with it the consciousness that powers

Green's formulation of "goodness" is thus closely akin to Kant's "categorical imperative" and there is no doubt that in this as in many other things he is indebted to the great German philosopher.

Morality is for Green a social value. This is indeed a necessary concept of political idealism, but Green is one of the few idealists who in advocating a social context for virtue is careful not to separate it from the individual. It is not simply a dictum by society or the state which makes an action moral, but also an individual's free assent after deliberation, which makes "a common good its own." [30] The road towards the achievement of this harmony between the individual and society is Hegelian in its character. First, the individual sees the social system surrounding him — the laws and institutions of his society and its conventional values. A mere passive acceptance of those cannot make the individual moral, since morality is not a passive acceptance of certain rules, but a "free," that is, rational act of the individual. Before the individual accepts conventional morality there is likely to occur in him a revolt against it. But barring a permanent revolt which results in stunting his moral growth he reverts eventually to the rules of society, but this time "freely" after a process of reflection. This final synthesis is the attainment of the "autonomy of will."

There are two assumptions about Green's "road to freedom." First that "a will is not really anything except the will of person, and, as we have seen, a will is not really determinable by anything foreign to itself . . ." [31] A modern psychologist would take a dim view of Green's formulation of the problem, and he could, indeed, find some support in what Green himself had to say about the role of "conventional morality."

The second assumption directly related to politics is the idea that society, any society, is moral in the sense, at least, of moving

---

should be so exercised; which means that there should be rights, that powers should be regulated by mutual recognition." *Ibid.*, p. 45.

[30] "The moral progress of mankind has no reality except as resulting in the formation of more perfect individual characters; but on the other hand every progress towards perfection on the part of the individual character presupposes some embodiment or expression of itself by the self-realizing principle in what may be called (to speak most generally) the organisation of life. It is in turn, however, only through the action of individuals that this organization of life is achieved." *Ibid.*, p. 24.

[31] *Ibid.*, p. 26.

towards the ideal of moral perfection, just in virtue of being a society. The critics of idealism grasp eagerly upon this statement as a proof that idealism preaches that "what is, is right." The criticism is justified insofar as Green's formulation of the immediate problem is concerned. It is not justified when the whole of his work is kept in mind. Perhaps Green was too much of a "pure" philosopher and too much under the spell of German idealism to realize that the relation of his general philosophy to his social philosophy was somewhat awkward. In his opening lines he attempts to deal with the problem, stating that, while the "highest morality" is attained through conventional morality, the latter being a "prior" and only partial embodiment of the idea has to be criticized from the point of view of the ideal.[32] While his work is thus a moral critique of political institutions, or a consideration of "what is of permanent moral value in the institutions of civil life, as established in Europe," the argument is somewhat delimited by the previous assumption that any society by being a society is "somewhat" moral.

An abstract discussion of freedom is hardly useful unless it is followed by an exposition of the actual rights of the citizen. Green rejects from the beginning the utilitarian basis for political rights and its antithesis, the theory of natural rights. The former he cannot accept for its philosophy is contrary to that of idealism; the latter is equally unacceptable since it postulates rights as prior to society.[33] Rights are social, they are the powers given by society to each individual to develop his moral personality and to contribute his best to society.

Green is not bothered by the thought that every society or every state may interpret in its own way the kind of rights which lead to "the moral disposition" on the part of its citizens. There is of course no theoretical barrier against state encroachment upon

[32] *Ibid.*, p. 30.

[33] "Political or civil rights, then, are not to be explained by derivation from natural rights, but in regard to both political and natural rights, in any sense in which there can be truly said to be natural rights, the question has to be asked, how it is that certain powers are recognized by men in their intercourse with each other as powers that should be exercised, or of which the possible exercise should be secured." *Ibid.*, p. 43.

civil liberty in the name of the highest ideals, but the concept of natural rights served for a long time as a useful myth enhancing the role of the individual. We need not go as far as certain liberal critics, who see in any claim that the state has a moral function a claim for its denial of rights to the citizen, to see certain flaws in Green's argument.

On the other hand Green's position enables him to see what the utilitarians failed to see: that the province of law is essentially limited, that positive law cannot enforce real morality, but can only set the most general barriers against antisocial behavior. It is only the outward acts that can be regulated by law while real morality proceeds from the inward will of the individual.[34] Green's position may appear to be an improvement only in style when compared with that of the utilitarians. Actually it is of great consequence for it gives him the basis to argue, as we shall see, that the real function of the state lies in creating the *conditions* for moral development of its citizens, rather than in enforcing it through law.[35]

Green's rephrasing of the problem of rights, his insistence that they are valuable only as the means for moral perfection, may lead a commentator to conclude that he limits individual freedom in favor of an undefinable ideal, which may easily be abused. A careful study of his work shows that he does nothing of the sort. The ideal is not an exaltation of the state, or of a religious creed, but a

[34] Ernest Barker contrasts Green's position with that of J. S. Mill. Mill tried to draw a rather hopeless division between self-regarding and other regarding actions while "Green makes a true distinction between outward actions necessary and valuable for the maintenance of rights — actions which the State can secure by external force because they are external — and actions proceeding from an inward will which are only valuable when they proceed from such a will and which therefore cannot be secured by any external force." E. Barker, *Political Thought in England, 1848–1914*, p. 54.

[35] "Have attempts ever been made by law to enforce acts as virtuous which lose their virtue when done under fear of legal penalties? . . . But without any strictly moral object at all, laws have been made which check the development of the moral disposition. This has been done (a) by legal requirements of religious observance and profession of belief, which, have tended to vitiate the religious source of morality; (b) by prohibitions and restraints, unnecessary, or which have ceased to be necessary, for maintaining the social conditions of the moral life . . . (c) by legal institutions which take away the occasion for the exercise of certain moral virtues . . ." Green, *Principles of Political Obligation*, pp. 38, 39.

free and moral citizen. And the writer gives us enough examples to show that what he means by his ideal is in no way repugnant to the democratic ideal.

The discussion of rights is an appropriate introduction to Green's concept of the state. It was said before that he conceived of the state as a political organization of society. More meaningfully he conceives the state as a protector and sponsor of the rights of its citizens, and he refuses to grant the title to a "state" which is a sheer tyranny, and which conceives its function otherwise.[36] It is a reasonable assumption that Green would agree that there must be an equality of rights, and that the sovereign power *as the agent of the society* is to protect those rights from without and within. The historian in Green is aware that, historically, states have come into being on a quite different basis — often through conquest — and that the actual institutions of a state are molded through the play of interests, or pressure groups as we would say today. But the philosopher insists that what creates the first approximation of the state is the idea of common and equal good translated into legal rights and what creates the "real" state is a considerable realization of the idea of equality.[37]

Green does not realize that despite his earlier denials he does in fact assume the concept of natural rights. His rights are "already existing" and the state gives only "fuller reality" to them. He is, to repeat, torn between two views — a necessary consequence of his attempt to reconcile Hegelian philosophy with that of individualism. The state is for him by definition an upholder of equal rights, yet a few pages later he admits ". . . actual states at best fulfil but partially their ideal function." [38] It follows that the state is a purposive organization of society. Its purpose is to secure equality and security of certain rights. If that purpose is not present, then Green

---

[36] ". . . state . . . is a body of persons recognized by each other as having rights and possessing certain institutions for the maintenance of those rights." *Ibid.*, p. 137.

[37] "In other words . . . a state is made a state by the functions which it fulfils of maintaining the rights of its members as a whole or a system in such a way that none gains at the expense of another, no one has any power guaranteed to him through another's being deprived of that power. Thus the state, or the sovereign as a characteristic institution of the state does not create rights, but gives fuller reality to rights already existing." *Ibid.*, p. 138.

[38] *Ibid.*, p. 148.

should consider the organization not as a state, but like Cicero or St. Augustine as a "band of robbers." Green could have saved himself his semantic troubles by saying what is implicit in his thought, that the democratic concept of the state is a dynamic one, that as long as the state has the idea of democracy as its purpose, as long as it moves towards its fulfillment, it is the type of state whose laws are to be obeyed by its citizens. If we adopt the definition we will not have solved any problems, but at least the discussion will shift from a problem of semantics to a more meaningful problem: what kind of social and political institutions should a democratic state have?

This question is discussed to some extent in the *Principles*. Green realizes, but insufficiently, that it is impossible to talk about politics without mentioning the materials of politics: social conditions, economic interests, various religious and national groupings. But the tendency is very strong in him to treat such problems as moral blemishes which the state "should" remove, without asking for their rationale or their remedies.[39]

A notable exception to a generally vague and sometimes ambiguous treatment of the more practical issues of politics is contained in the chapters entitled "The Right of the State to Promote Morality" and "The Right of the State in Regard to Property." In these two chapters Green's political philosophy is used to probe the actual institutions of the state. The passages indicated are most important for his political views, and they also mark the turning point in English social philosophy.

The whole system of laissez faire was being questioned in Green's lifetime by a handful of philosophers and writers. But

[39] A typical case of such treatment is his discussion of the causes of war: "Remove from European states, as they are and have been during the last hundred years, the occasions of apparently competing interests, which arise in one or other of the ways mentioned, either from the mistaken view of state interests which a privileged class inevitably takes, or from the presence in them of oppressed populations, or from what we improperly call the antagonism of religious confessions — and there would not be or have anything to disturb the peace between them. And this is to say that the source of war between states lies in their incomplete fulfilment of their function; in the fact that there is some defect in the maintenance or reconciliation of rights among their subjects." *Ibid.*, p. 171. One can say: amen to that, but the prescription begs many questions. What makes a state defective in its "maintenance of rights" and what kind of machinery will remedy the defect?

protests against it were being voiced by people like Carlyle or Ruskin who proceeded, in general, from an authoritarian tradition and reflected a romantic dislike of the modern industrial civilization. Mill tells us in his autobiography that his conversion to socialism came largely as the result of disillusionment with the possibilities of purely political democracy. It is only Green in that generation who makes his critique of the extremes of laissez faire wholly consistent with his general political philosophy, and to whom it comes not as an afterthought or a result of broken illusions, but as the logical conclusion of a philosophical position.

The principle is that the state as a "hinderer of hindrances" should enable the individual to enjoy his rights, thus enabling him to have a "capacity for spontaneous action regulated by a conception of common good." [40] Yet the state cannot fulfill this obligation if it refrains in practice and in theory from interfering with certain private rights which indirectly lead to poverty, bad health, and lack of educational facilities on the part of many of its citizens. The widespread abolition of various state restraints upon private dealings which from the end of the eighteenth century until the end of the nineteenth signified the triumphant emergence of the middle class as the ruling class was not, according to Green, an unmixed blessing.[41] Green is here not only a philosopher but an observer of social conditions, and his thinking is in itself a symptom of the vast change in the climate of opinion soon to take place. His thought is not a continuation of the tradition of Conservative paternalism of Shaftesbury and Sadler, but an extension of his idea that democracy implies a measure of equality going beyond the ballot box and spilling into the social and economic conditions of society. Professor Dicey characterized the period in which Green

---

[40] *Ibid.*, p. 208.

[41] "In the hurry of removing those restraints on free dealing between man and man, which have arisen partly perhaps from some confused idea of maintaining morality, but much more from the power of class interests, we have been apt to take too narrow a view of the range of persons — not one generation merely, but succeeding generations whose freedom ought to be taken into account, and of the conditions necessary to their freedom (freedom here meaning their qualification for their exercise of rights). Hence the massing of population without regard to conditions of health; unrestrained traffic in deleterious commodities; unlimited upgrowth of the class of hired labourers in particular industries which circumstances have suddenly stimulated, without any provision against the danger of an impoverished proletariate in following generations." *Ibid.*, pp. 209–210.

wrote, the period beginning with the Education Act of 1870, as the beginning of a collectivist era in British legislation,[42] and though in our eyes this collectivism appears of an infinitely mild variety, Green's thought is certainly symptomatic of the change.

Green criticized Rousseau on the ground that the latter in his quest for the General Will and majorities loses sight of what really ought to be enacted by the state to promote common welfare. Yet he himself falls short on this count. He approves of compulsory education;[43] but when it comes to the question of property in general and the ground on which the state can interfere with it, he is full of doubts. He leans towards a law that would require equal inheritance among a proprietor's children and thus break up the great landed estates of England. Likewise certain restrictions should be placed upon free use of land by its owner.

The whole problem of property is approached somewhat diffidently. He is very much impressed by the standard arguments for private property stated with their peculiar variations by Aristotle, Locke, and Hegel. It is characteristic that he probes most deeply into the question of *property in land* and touches but incidentally upon industrial problems of the age. Capitalism is for him still a beneficent force; the existence of the proletariat and the conditions of urban life should be blamed on English feudalism, which has passed into "unrestrained landlordism." [44] There is a limit to the extent a man can tear himself away from the atmosphere of his age, and in directing his scrutiny of private property almost exclusively to landed property Green follows in the tradition of Ricardo, J. S. Mill, and Bright; in the tradition of a long line of liberal theorists and practical politicians for whom the problem appeared in this guise.

The type of political theory found in *The Principles of Political Obligation* has seldom an immediate or direct influence on political life. With all their ambiguities, hesitations, and contradictions Green's ideas are, nevertheless, symptomatic of their times and seminal insofar as the later development of English political

[42] A. V. Dicey, *Law and Public Opinion in England during the 19th Century* (London, 1905).
[43] Green, *Principles*, p. 209.
[44] *Ibid.*, p. 228.

thought is concerned. They appear at the point of exhaustion (as we see it now but hardly obvious in the 1870's) of the victory of liberal principles in English politics. The age of reform launched in 1832 was still going on, but indications were appearing perceptibly that not all of the hopes associated with its inception were to be fulfilled. Some of Green's contemporaries — the Christian Socialists and Ruskin and Carlyle — expressed their dislike of the industrial society which ushered in and intertwined itself with the principles of laissez faire and political liberalism. Others like Lecky and Maine questioned the whole rationale of the advance towards democracy. For Green political democracy was a moral necessity. He saw that underlying political rights there must be a modicum of social and economic equality, in the sense at least of what we would call today equality of opportunity. The state was obviously the only instrument capable of insuring the reforms needed to bring about that measure of equality. Hence he suggests that the state may have to interfere with the freedom of contract and has to play a positive role insofar as education is concerned. These proposals, along with the suggestions that the whole system of land tenure ought to be reëxamined, strike us as being incongruously mild when set against Green's original thesis. Within the context of the times the reforms advocated appear as a notable and well-thought-out advance on the question of how the state can by positive action promote social and economic improvements.

The general contribution of Green to political thought is so much bound up with that of idealism that it cannot be adequately discussed aside from a critique of the whole movement. A few comments can, however, be anticipated. Much can be said for and against the proposition that a discussion of morals and Christian ethics does not really belong to the realm of politics, or at least that it is dangerous to base one's political conclusions solely upon moral precepts. Is there really such a thing as "the state"? Does an average citizen really conceive it to be his duty to revolt against an "immoral state"? To such questions there is no simple answer. It is clear on the other hand that a plea for democracy must be anchored in some moral, a priori belief, for if we look at the history of mankind as a whole there seems to be, otherwise, not much ground for such a belief. Those who have ignored that fact and based their theories upon utilitarian, positivistic, or pragmatic deductions, do not escape the suspicion that beneath the varnish of their "science" they conceal the same basic belief. Green spells out his basic beliefs. Furthermore, for all his naïveté on the issues of economics and practical politics, he sees, perhaps accidentally, the type of problems to which a free nation must address itself if it is to continue and to develop as a democracy. It may be that he simply feels the needs of the hour and the problems of the future, and dresses them into an abstract philosophical form — but that, after all, is the job of a political theorist.

It can be argued that Green's approach is pure rhetoric. But he gives enough examples of practical political and social issues to disprove the charge. He grasps for a concept of democracy and gives a few examples to show that only through democracy can the elusive goal of personal freedom be reconciled with the existence of the state. It is paradoxical but true that for Green the free development of human personality cannot be the end of social progress unless it is also the means through which this progress is achieved.

FRANCIS HERBERT BRADLEY

Bradley occupies a much larger place in the history of British philosophy than does Green. In contrast Bradley's role as a *political* philosopher is much more limited. He contributed what is, at most, a preface to political theory, a single essay. The title of the essay seems, in itself, to promise a version of *The Republic's* view of the individual in society and a conclusion of Hegel's social philosophy: "My Station and Its Duties." Bradley, a man who led a solitary academic life, cut off even from that intense preoccupation with social problems which characterized the lives of Green and Bosanquet, was par excellence a pure philosopher. His importance in political idealism lies largely in the influence he had on Bosanquet.

"My Station and Its Duties" is at the same time a vivid example of the type of political idealism most heavily attacked by its critics. That short essay, part of Bradley's *Ethical Studies*, contains the statement which appears on the surface as the essence of conservative, if not reactionary, dogma in the tradition of Burke or Hegel: the individual is unalterably inferior to society, his place and functions are fixed by it, and he should not try to change them.[45] The whole idea of an exaltation of the community to the point where individual preferences are considered unimportant appears clearly antithetical to the democratic creed.

A certain degree of caution is demanded, however, before we consign Bradley to the antidemocratic camp. To use a farfetched analogy, we see today many enlightened people who are fervent believers in individual freedom and who at the same time plead for a world government or an international organization approaching it as much as possible. Should a world state or something approaching it materialize, should it become, as it well might despite all the "constitutions" and precautions, an oppressive growth unmindful of the claims of national groups and of individual freedom, the present protagonists of a world organization would appear to the future as the ideologists and precursors of tyranny. It is likewise unfair to label the emphasis on the community and disparagement of individualism as such, as certain marks of a reactionary philosophy. Bradley's philosophy is, as we shall see, uncongenial to many points of the liberal and democratic dogma, but the reason for it does not lie primarily in his insistence that the individual finds his fulfillment in working for and in the spirit of his community.

Bradley is often characterized as a Neo-Hegelian in contrast to Green — a Neo-Kantian. It is difficult to understand the insistence upon the prefix in Bradley's case. His treatment of the problem of the state is Hegelian, both in its attitude and in its phraseology. Since his writings on political philosophy are limited, he lacks, of course, the complexity, the richness and poetry of Hegel. Furthermore, the English philosopher does not follow his master in elucidating the difference between the state and society. The weight of tradition results in a confusion of the two concepts, and there is a real question whether Bradley does not, in fact, identify the General Will — the moral idea — embodied in the state with the body of beliefs and opinions accepted by society.

The rejection of individualism proceeds from Bradley's dislike of both the utilitarian idea of society as a mere sum of autonomous

[45] ". . . at present we may take it as an obvious fact that in my station my particular duties are prescribed to me and I have them whether I wish to or not." Bradley, p. 176.

individuals, and from his disapproval of moral individualism per se which he calls the theory of "duty for duty's sake." It is difficult not to see in the latter a rephrasing of Kant's position seen also in Green's political philosophy. The alternative position of "my station and its duties" sees the individual as an organic part of his society. Bradley adds an anthropological note to a philosophical formulation of the problem in saying that society really lives within each of us through heredity and the whole complex of social influences.[46] Man cannot be taken in isolation, but as a member of a "system of wholes" culminating in the state. Thus a man aside from his position in society is meaningless.

Bradley's view on the question deserves the comment of Laski on Bosanquet: ". . . to say that I am however largely influenced by my relations is not to say that I am my relations." [47] But Bradley carries the point to an extreme, asserting that aside from his society an individual cannot realize moral law at all, because the latter has no particular content without a social context.[48] What Bradley ignores is the obvious point that even if we reject the theory of innate moral ideas, we have a variety of religious and philosophical systems as well as a vast historical experience to help us set moral standards, which may be quite contrary to those of the society in which we live. For him, however, it is only our position in the community which makes us moral in the sense that the "universal" becomes (a) concrete, (b) objective, and (c) leaves nothing of us outside it. To be moral one has, in short, to acquiesce in the character of society and one's own position in it.

Reading such sentiments today one may be drawn to the conclusion that Bradley excluded the possibility of social change and reform, and that no society but one in a condition of stagnation under a dictatorship would fit his prescription. In the context of the last quarter of the nineteenth century Bradley's position meant essentially the insistence on national community against the claims of excessive individualism, and a strong sense of unity and mutual

[46] *Ibid.*, p. 173. Yet aside, perhaps, from a very primitive society, the variety of hereditary social and cultural influences contributes to vastly different behavior of different individuals. The state according to Hegel possesses the higher unity and reality exactly because society is too amorphous and differentiated. It is to be suspected that Hegelian philosophy and anthropology don't mix.

[47] *Proceedings of the Aristotelian Society*, Suppl., VIII (London, 1928), 50.

[48] Bradley, p. 176.

interdependence of society. It is easy against the background of recent history to read in the words written in 1876 a dangerous message for today, but due consideration for the historical background does not allow such an abrupt judgment.

Bradley allows rather naïvely for the possibility that a community may become corrupted so that it represents no longer the moral ideal but the sheer idea of compulsion.[49] It is characteristic of his whole approach that he does not dwell upon the point; nor does he describe the criteria of corruption. Green hesitated whether to classify Tsarist Russia as a "state," and we may assume a parallel though unspoken conviction on the part of Bradley: that a despotic state cannot lay claim to the allegiance of its citizens.

The question of Bradley's political convictions is rather submerged in his philosophical statement of the meaning of the state. We run continually into the problem of semantics when we encounter terms which meant one thing to Hegel, which acquire a different meaning in Bradley's England, and which to us have a rather grating sound reminiscent not so much of philosophical ideas but of recent and unfortunate events. The state is for Bradley, following Hegel's classic definition, a synthesis of despotism and individualism. Individualism is defined as that intense development of personality and participation on the part of individual citizens in common life without which the state becomes ossified. We seem to have, for a moment, a typical prescription for a modern dictatorship with its machinery for indoctrination, for keeping the citizen continually active in contrast to the ancient despot who was content to have his subjects passive and terrified. But the implication is unwarranted, for "despotism" is defined simply as the imperative that every citizen should participate to the fullest in the community's life.[50] Actually Bradley's "individualism" and "despotism" come to mean the same thing: the individual has to discharge his function in life with the thought of and for his community or the state. The old concept of autonomous individuals working for their own ends and brought into harmony only by an "unseen hand" is banished. In its place we have an equally extravagant notion of "the spirit of the community" which men should imbibe "by precept and still more by example."

[49] *Ibid.*, p. 203.
[50] *Ibid.*, p. 188.

Views of such nature are often described as conservative and perhaps justly so. But implicit in Bradley's theories, and indeed in all the writings of the idealists, is something critics of the school have missed. Bradley accepts by definition the type of government England has developed. While he does not condescend to talk about concrete political facts, his very insistence upon the spirit and mores of the community, his Burke-like distaste of change except by evolution, makes it impossible to construe his theory as running against the notion of the form of government current in his time in England. His philosophy is that of "progress" in Burke's sense of the word; it makes him accept the contemporary society and the very fact which makes him a conservative prevents him from being a reactionary.

The repeated mention of Burke is not accidental. There are passages in Bradley's short essay that might have been written by Burke (had the latter foreseen nineteenth-century German philosophy!). The aspect of individualism most disliked by Bradley is John Stuart Mill's notion of the creative power of individual ideas. For Bradley the only safe route for a reformer is to start from generally accepted ideas and in harmony with the general spirit of the community (whatever that means) and to build from them a better world. But it is wrong to start from the ideals "in one's head" and to oppose them to the state and society.[51] There is an unconscious humor in Bradley's formulation of the problem for there is no doubt that the type of political philosophy at which he hinted was far from being "in the spirit of the community," while the very theory which he decried was the ruling, if declining, political tradition in England of his day.

The paradox illuminates the main difficulty in Bradley's theory. Read in the context of its times "My Station and Its Duties" is not a negation of democracy. Dressed up in different phraseology the main points — his denial of extreme individualism, his insistence that the community is the source of our moral ideas and their only arbiter, his concept of the state as a moral idea rather than a utilitarian machine — all could be incorporated into the democratic or even latter-day liberal creed. His theory does not deliver the individual tied hand and foot to an arbitrary state.

[51] *Ibid.*, p. 200.

The notion is still implicit that the best interests of the state and of the free individual coincide, and the only thing which Bradley adds is the need for a heightened social awareness for a more complete association in society and the state. Yet this very confidence that the future holds no threat of a frankly despotic state, inimical to the moral interests of its citizens, leads him to define the problem in a way that is self-contradictory — from the point of view of idealism. Furthermore it leads him to a postulate that in its implications is certainly anti-intellectual and antiliberal. He accepts what might be called unreasoning and unqualified pragmatism in denying the usefulness of theoretical discussion of politics beyond accepting the given stage of society at its face value.[52] Such a notion is suicidal to a political philosopher. There is some justice in holding that the primary duty of a political philosopher is to see what is happening to the state and society rather than to build utopias. But the whole notion of idealism as elucidated by Hegel is that society is a growing and developing organism, and that each of the phases of its development is meaningful only if we appraise it against its genesis in the past and its consequence in the future. Furthermore, human society is not a monolithic whole. To order philosophy and philosophers to limit their investigation just to finding out "what is" is absurd for we can never answer the question without understanding "what is elsewhere" and, ultimately, without stating "what should be."

Bradley's position is more than a reaction to the rationalism and individualism which since the eighteenth century have dominated British political thought. It is characteristic of his confusion that in the passages where he tries to expel reason from the realm of social action he comes close to negating the basic assumption of idealism.[53] The passive acceptance of society, its mores and customs, is a negation of the idea of the state. The element of "free-

---

[52] "The non-theoretical person if he be not immoral is at peace with reality and the man who in any degree has made this point of view his own becomes more and more reconciled to the world and to life, and the theories of 'advanced thinkers' come to him more and more as the thinnest and most miserable abstractions." *Ibid.*, p. 184.

[53] E. g., "If a man is to know what is right he should have imbibed by precept and still more by example the spirit of his community, its general and special beliefs as to right and wrong, and with this whole embodied in his mind, should particularize it in any new case, not by a reflective deduction, but by an intuitive subsumption, which does not know it is subsumption." *Ibid.*, p. 196.

dom" in the Hegelian system is not a fiction; it stands for the ability to tear oneself away from the confines of social opinion and to set up an ideal, and a dynamic ideal at that, embodied in the state. The whole history of the concept of the state, whether we adopt or reject idealism, shows a progression from the form of a political organization of society to an organ imposing certain ideals upon society and coercing some sections of it in the name of those ideals. To see society as the fulfillment of the individual, to demand of his actions that they be for *social good* is one thing. To demand of the individual that his personality should become merged in the social whole and that his thinking become "an intuitive subsumption" is another and manifestly absurd postulate. It finds its fulfillment only in a most primitive society.

Bradley's political philosophy ends, therefore, in a blind alley of self-contradiction. But the effort itself remains instructive. It shows the danger in a political philosophy separated from political theory, the danger in trying to prescribe the rules of political and social behavior without trying to see what the general facts of social and political behavior are. More significantly Bradley's failure illuminates the usual failure of a theoretician when he tries to understand the phenomenon of the state or society without a specific purpose in mind. Bradley is inferior as a *political* philosopher to Green for exactly that reason. One-sided and therefore limited as the political philosophy of Green is, it has in common with such great viewpoints of politics as those of Rousseau, Bentham, and Marx the great illuminating power of a social purpose which, though making it vulnerable to attack, gives it the advantage of being tangible and constructive. Bradley's philosophy is on the other hand, at best, a preface to politics. It is valuable insofar as it shows the confusion between the state and society, and the confusion between reason and "public opinion." Democratic theory of the state must clear away this confusion if it is to advance beyond rhetoric.

BERNARD BOSANQUET'S PHILOSOPHICAL THEORY OF THE STATE

It has been said before that a criticism of idealism in terms suggested here is in a sense unfair. What appears today to us to be quibbling over words and violent agitation over the issues with which we are quite familiar and which no longer startle us, was for Green and Bradley an important matter of principle to be established over the hitherto dominant tradition of extreme individualism and utilitarianism. It is likewise necessary to keep in mind the background against which the new theory was being projected. The map of Europe in the 1870's lost its fluid and unstable character with the crystallization of great national states. Great movements of reform and reaction were being transformed from sporadic and revolutionary activities into well-organized parties. The liberal theory and the liberal movement in general found themselves in the position of the sorcerer's apprentice, having unleashed or helped to unleash the forces which they could not control. Having destroyed the vestiges of feudalism and having set the modern state on the road towards full political participation by the masses, liberalism found itself unable to control the movement. The resources of a political theory are never adequate to cope with the situation which arises when its postulates have been realized, but its prophecies have remained unfulfilled, and the basic assumptions of the theory concerning human behavior if not proven false have been thrown in doubt. The realities of party politics, of narrow and militant nationalism, and of class conflicts — they all accompanied the undoubted democratization of political life in Western Europe, and at the threshold of the new century confronted the orthodox liberal doctrine with awkward dilemmas.

The challenge was reflected in the realm of theory. It is a truism to say that liberalism relies on the tradition of rationalism and individualism. In Western thought this tradition is almost an intangible thing and various attempts to define the two concepts have failed to reproduce the effect of the accretion of ideas and institutional devices designed to assure men that they are rational because they can manage their own affairs, and that they are free because they are rational. The new century was to present this pleasing circular reasoning as a possible optical illusion and to suggest that progress or the triumph of man over history was not a necessary adjunct of the growth of society but a more or less accidental occurrence connected with the favorable condition of the West during the nineteenth century. The forces which were to be unleashed in the twentieth century had been gathering before and a variety of theories heralded their "appearance" and the disturbing effect they had upon the hitherto complacent and un-self-conscious atmosphere of liberalism.

Strangely enough socialism did not appear as the most disturbing competitor of liberalism. To an intellectual who in 1900 essayed various theories of society and government, socialism even in its Marxian variety may have appeared as a logical extension of the liberal tradition. Its radicalism and dogmatic sharpness were reminiscent of the early stages of liberal thought. And in the same tradition socialism appeared already softening its theory and susceptible of a compromise with life and ready to be fitted into the pattern of a Western parliamentary state.

Much more disturbing from the point of view of a man whose intellectual background included Smith, Bentham, and Mill, was a trend not backed by a growing political movement, but found with an increased frequency in writers of various nationalities. The trend was distinct from the main tradition of Western political thought, to wit, that man is a rational hence a political animal. Now a variety of philosophical and sociological doctrines began to impinge upon the tradition. The theories of William James, Bergson, Durkheim, to mention a few, provided a certain atmosphere of *fin de siècle*. They were not without their influence upon the theories of Sorel and Pareto, which were to bear more directly upon the matters of politics. As the main philosophical tenets of liberalism were being questioned directly and by implication, it is not strange that the minutiae of the political apparatus of democracy — parliaments and parties — were soon to be subjected to scrutiny by people like Ostrogorski and Michels. The galaxy of names can be expanded by many other examples. But it is easy to see that we are no longer dealing with occasional doubters and critics of whom we spoke before in discussing certain parts of the philosophies of Mill and Green. The trend of which we speak is a widespread philosophical movement which in the twenty years preceding the First World War penetrated all sphere of social and intellectual activity. It is only fair to say that the cumulative effect of these various currents of thought was not a new and vigorous social and political creed but a certain exhaustion of the older creed. It is sometimes argued that intellectuals are perverse creatures who live by nibbling at the foundations of the existing system and scoffing at the accepted doctrine. Yet it is possible to assume that they express in part, at least, the spirit of their times, that a widespread intellectual movement of the nature described above reflects the changed mood of a whole society.

What characterizes the work of Bernard Bosanquet is exactly this awareness of a period of transition in political philosophy. His *Philosophical Theory of the State*[54] is a restatement of political idealism, but it is at the same time a running commentary on contemporary political trends. The work as a whole has a comprehensiveness and an awareness of conflicting political and philosophical opinions which give it a supreme importance in modern political thought. Bosanquet is both a political theorist and a political analyst. The latter quality is of a somewhat academic variety — he analyzes acutely theories and institutions rather than life. But recurrent in his philosophy is the idea of synthesis, of restoration of the theory of the state, which he believes the modern world inherited from the Greeks and which found its expression in the school of idealism, both German and British. This theory, based on rationalism and a belief in the organic unity of the individual with his society, is threatened by various "sociological" and irrationalist tendencies of modern thought. The tendencies themselves express the inherent danger of a breakdown of the modern state. Behind them lurk the dangers of nihilism and class warfare. Hence, the "right" theory of the state has to be reëstablished: the state is to be shown as a necessary implementation of man's personality. Without it there is no role for the individual to play. The concepts of economic classes, of material interests, of irrational impulses guiding man, can all be absorbed by the classical theory of the state as long as its central point remains a social orientation of man, which in turn depends upon the faculty of human mind to merge all the environmental and biological influences in a concept of itself and its society.[55]

It follows, therefore, that Bosanquet's task is different from that

[54] London, 1899 and 1910. Quotations in text from the second edition.

[55] Bosanquet uses a happy phrase in attacking the purely environmental viewpoint which he attributes with some justice to the Marxists. "The world in which man lives is himself, but is constituted, of course, by presentation to a mind and not by strictly physical causation." *Philosophical Theory of the State,* p. 31.

of Green. The latter was mainly interested in seeing what rights the community — the state — could hold over its citizens and in return what was incumbent upon the community to do for the individual. It is paradoxical but nevertheless accurate to say that Green could criticize the reigning doctrine of political and economic individualism because he took so many of its assumptions for granted. No significant body of thought in England at the time of the *Lectures on the Principles of Political Obligation* questioned the basis of human rationality or refused to acquiesce in a theory of progress. The rumblings of the Romantics, of Carlyle and Ruskin, were behind, if not in time then in influence and importance.[56]

Bosanquet's book appears on the other hand in a decade when the liberal theory is strongly under attack from many sources. On the surface his book is not concerned with a defence of the liberal creed as such. His main interest is to defend the notion of the community as a moral organism and to disparage the relativism which creeps into social theory. The displacement of liberalism as the reigning doctrine resulted in a "neosophism." The *Philosophical Theory of the State* is one long pamphlet against the "neo-Sophists" among whom Bosanquet would count both the socialists and the sociological school of his day. The result is that Bosanquet's work has little appeal to a modern liberal. On social issues, he maintains, as he puts it, an uncontroversial position. The whole work lacks the passionate, if somewhat vague, preoccupation with social justice which characterizes Green's writings and which makes him, to a superficial critic, an example of a "good" idealist in contradistinction to Bosanquet — a "bad" idealist always preoccupied with rehashing Hegel and sacrificing the individual at the "altar of the state." The truth is that Bosanquet was not unmindful of social problems and of economic reform and in his personal views was certainly far from being a reactionary.[57] Whether rightly or wrongly he considered the problem of the state and its nature as the focal point of any political theory. If the state could not be shown to be more than a mechanical aggregate of individuals, if

---

[56] As for writers like Bagehot, Lecky, and Maine, it is doubtful whether they opposed in principle the assumptions stated above.

[57] After the First World War his sympathies extended towards the Labour Party. See Muirhead, *Bernard Bosanquet and His Friends*, p. 217.

there were no precise moral obligations flowing from an association in the state, then there was no sense in initiating programs of reform and reconstruction. Before showing what the state should do it is necessary to show what the state is.

It is only natural that in the consideration of the problem the ghosts of Rousseau and Hegel should occupy the stage. Mention was made before of the curious fact that any discussion of the state in English political thought is likely to confuse its nature with that of society or of government. Hence the attraction of Rousseau and Hegel to anybody who wants to pose the question. Both of these thinkers differentiate sharply between society and the state. Both of them take the state as a moral institution endowed with will and therefore life while society is in contrast rather inert — an accidental arrangement of family, of economic and professional interests and relationships. The distinction, on this score, between the two writers was that Rousseau combined his separate-from-society state with a passionate democratic belief which led him to negate the legitimacy of any but direct democracy as the basis of the moral state. Bosanquet is compelled to reject this definition of the state, as it is quite impractical under modern conditions. He uses Rousseau's own concept of the Legislator to point out that while the state is separate from society, it is in a sense the product of the latter and that real General Will may be found not so much in the wills of the citizens all thrown together at periodic intervals, but in the spirit and working of the "habits and institutions of any community." [58] Thus constitutionalism and representative democracy find their niche in Bosanquet's own theory of the General Will. Society through its institutions sets the tone of the state. The latter in turn as a conscious organism imparts its will to the citizens, and makes what is implicit in social institutions explicit in daily life.

This rather obtuse concept is really necessary as a preliminary assumption for a widespread social and economic activity by the state. The search for peace and justice is inherent in human nature. (Here we are again following Rousseau.) What obscures this element of human nature is society, which by its nature is divided into groups and factions with their own parochial and professional interests. The state on the contrary is all-embracing and superior

[58] *Philosophical Theory of the State,* p. 123.

to any group, and therefore it is only in a purely political relationship that men can be free, as it is this relationship which removes
the ties of sentiment and interest which produce personal and
group selfishness.[59]

There is an inherent difficulty in construing Rousseau's theory
the way Bosanquet does it. The notion of the Legislator which he
emphasizes is after all of secondary importance in Rousseau's plan.
Bosanquet gives it such a prominent place because it fits in with
his historical and institutional interpretation of the General Will.
The latter is no longer a spontaneous and genuine expression of a
people unencumbered with a highly complicated society. Bosanquet's General Will is more akin to the "spirit of the nation" which
is found not in the actual decision making by the people but rather
in the history and character of the institutions. It is Rousseau
tempered by Burke if not by Hegel, and there is no doubt that a
theory of this kind by its emphasis upon the past, and its hints of
an evolutionary process, is in general conservative.

That characteristic comes to life most vividly when Bosanquet
discusses what he calls "Neighbourhood." The concept itself and
its discussion are veiled in a sort of Victorian sentimentality, but
there can be no doubt that he opposes the concept of the state to
that of the neighborhood. The modern state unlike the Greek city-
state does not come into being until it has ceased to be a neighborhood. While this is historically correct it is completely opposed to
Rousseau's ideas on the subject. The latter wanted his state to be
a "neighborhood," and denied to a great centralized nation-state
any beneficent effects on its citizens. It has long been pointed out
that one of the sources of modern totalitarianism has been the
attempt to impose the type of uniformity of public opinion and
sentiment which supposedly comes spontaneously in a small community upon a great nation-state where it has to be done by law,
hence often by coercion. It might be observed parenthetically that

---

[59] "The General Will seems to be, in the last resort, the ineradicable impulse
of an intelligent being to a good extending beyond itself, in as far as that good takes
the form of a common good." *Ibid.*, p. 109. Rousseau was of course aware that the
craving for power, even if unconnected with economic motives, can be the most
powerful incentive for selfishness. The form and nature of the state he erects
would guarantee against this abuse. Those who follow him, but who reject, like
Bosanquet, his specific prescriptions, have neglected this aspect of the problem.

the whole idea of the inherent virtue and purity of a small community is rather naïve. The persistence of the myth started by Rousseau from his admiration of the Greek city-state is amazing: it has colored idealistic thought down to this day, as observed in the thought of A. D. Lindsay; it is one of the central motives in pluralism; and perhaps even the American myth of the evils of "bigness" in business as contrasted with the undoubted virtue of a small businessman may be in a way traced back to the romantic ideas of Rousseau. In Bosanquet's own scheme the admiration for a small community life is quite evident. But it is subordinated to a theory of the nation-state as the highest organ demanding the fullest loyalty of the citizen.

The theory of the state does not come naturally to an English writer; even less natural is the idea of the nation-state. Great Britain has been, in modern times, a multination state, and there is of course the Empire. Yet Bosanquet retains the double noun since he is eager to retain as much of Rousseau's theory as possible. There has to be a common bond uniting the citizens, and this bond must be founded upon a certain similarity of cultural background. The idea is not developed very elaborately and there is no hint of cultural or national exclusiveness in the discussion.[60] "Nation-State" is used mostly to distinguish a modern state from a city-state or other "incomplete" forms of political organization.

The pitfalls of a theory of the state are always encountered when the theory faces a concrete problem of life. In brief what is the nature of the state's actions? Are they to be judged by the criteria applicable to individual acts?

Rousseau solved the problem thus: if the General Will is operative, if a state is the kind of state he prescribed, then the General Will — the state — cannot be wrong in its decisions. If the "judgment" of the sovereign people is corrupted, then we have no General Will. The problem of injustice and oppression by the people themselves simply does not exist if human nature had been freed from the shackles of corrupting institutions. There is thus no middle ground between corruption and perfection.

The classic liberal position has always been that the state has no particular claim to escape a judgment of its actions on the same

---

[60] See *ibid.*, pp. 321–322.

terms which are applied to private persons and institutions. The state is not a metaphysical abstraction nor a superhuman body: it is simply one of many institutions with a locus of responsibility clearly fixed.[61] The state and its agents are invested with no particular sanctity, insofar as they are political and not symbolic in their nature.

It is easy to see that such an attitude is in a sense crucial to the liberal theory, especially in Great Britain and the United States. Strictly speaking orthodox liberalism has no theory of the state. The idealists' mythical and metaphysical formulation of the state corresponds to the attributes liberalism bestows upon something variously called constitutionalism or government of laws. Due to its historical setting the liberalism of Bentham and the Mills viewed the doctrines of "state reason," "national interest," and so forth, with great suspicion. Due to its philosophical foundations the liberalism of the utilitarians was (and in general liberalism has remained) something of an iconoclastic doctrine and even the principle of constitutionalism mentioned above never commanded the reverence which the state inspired in the idealists. It can be claimed that the liberal view is a necessary one if we are solicitous to preserve and augment individual liberties. It can be seen also that taken in its strict application the disparagement of the state handicaps a political theory which would combine individual freedom with great plans of social welfare and reconstruction sponsored by government. Likewise the spirit of iconoclasm whispers into the ears of one type of liberal that whenever his state follows a resolute and forceful line of foreign policy, its government is of necessity bent upon aggrandizement and extending its power rather than the defence of the common interest.

Bosanquet's own position marks a complete departure from the liberal doctrine of the nature of the state. He goes much farther than Green, for whom state actions had to be scrutinized according to moral standards and sometimes when they did not pass the test

[61] Some writers have tried to relate this theoretical question to the issue of administrative justice and the accountability of a state for the acts of its officials. Without going into the subject it is interesting to point out the contrast between the views of, say, Dicey, who insisted that there was no system of administrative law in England, and the reality of today when the British practice can no longer be pointed out as the exact opposite of the elaborate French system of administrative courts and rules.

they were to be resisted by a moral citizen even though a majority should have acquiesced in them. For Bosanquet the state can hardly do wrong. No criteria of private morality can be applied to state actions.[62] The state is the highest moral organization in absence of an organized world community. The action of the state is by its nature always concerned with the broadest interest of its citizens. More than that it is the trustee and the agency through which mankind develops (Bosanquet hesitates whether to say progresses). In view of such a "higher" nature of the state, the adjectives used to describe private actions are simply irrelevant. The state is a greater "self"; it cannot be judged by the criteria of morality suitable to the actions of individuals. Nor can we judge the state, strictly speaking, on the basis of a popular approval of its actions. The state is like a work of art: in a sense a product of society, but concretely the work of some particular people, it can be appreciated by some but not by all. In a passage devoted to "art, philosophy, and religion" [63] Bosanquet emphasizes that they are creations of human spirit and the inheritance of all, but that it does not follow that they are social in the sense of being fashioned to meet the needs of all the people. The General Will, he said elsewhere, is too subtle a thing to be fully interpreted at the ballot box. Thus in a true Hegelian fashion the state becomes something separate from actual human volition and approbation. For the first time in English political philosophy (for Bradley's effort is not, after all, an elaborated political theory) we meet the concept of perfection and fulfillment of the process of history *outside* of individual conscience and mind.

The theory of such a sort can be criticized or extolled. The dangers inherent in it may be pointed out, and the analogy drawn with various totalitarian concepts. But it is more important to see what Bosanquet is trying to do, and what, concretely, his theory of the state was supposed to serve.

In speaking about the "sociological theory" Bosanquet objected

[62] "The State, then, exists to promote good life, and what it does cannot be morally indifferent; but its actions cannot be identified with the deeds of its agents, or morally judged as private volitions are judged. Its acts proper are always public acts, and it cannot, as a State act within the relations of private life in which organized morality exists." *Ibid.*, p. 324.

[63] *Ibid.*, p. 333.

strongly to Durkheim's definition of crime as an act which merely "offends the strong and definite collective sentiments of society." [64] The sociologist's theory would equate crime with the reaction of anger provoked in a group or a mob. To Bosanquet this means an introduction of complete relativism into the realm of moral judgment. Under such a definition there are no absolute values — there are no morals — only the public opinion. There are points of value in the sociological theory; it avoids the emptiness and formality of a pure legal theory as envisaged by John Austin. But neither sociology nor the "command" type of theory of jurisprudence offers an achor to which the modern man can affix his standard of values. Both theories do, in effect, emerge from scepticism, from the flux and uncertainty of modern life. In formulating his theory of the state Bosanquet offers an ideal and a standard of values. Man, being a social being, does not find his realization in the fullest development of his individuality, though this should be a by-product of a worthwhile social system. Self-fulfillment can be found only in various social organizations of which the state is the highest. The obsession with the state does not proceed from a liking for authoritarianism or nationalism, but from the conviction that man's duty lies in service to his fellow human beings and in striving for self-perfection, and that the state stands for both of these ideas.

Any and every state? There are hints in *Philosophical Theory of the State* that there is no true political obligation under a despotic government.[65] Nor would Bosanquet go along with the theories which would represent the community as invariably infallible in its actions affecting the individual. But where is the borderline of political obedience, and where are the tokens of a "true" state? No political theory has answered these questions and in a sense they are unanswerable. If, as we saw Bosanquet affirm, the state cannot be judged by the ordinary standard of morals then it can hardly be judged at all. If we hesitate to assign the task of judging the state's performance to the majority of its citizens, then we have no judge. We find that we have affixed our values to some-

[64] *Ibid.*, p. 37.
[65] See chap. iii, "The Paradox of Political Obligation: Self-Government."

thing which can hardly be defined, and which cannot be criticized or evaluated.

The whole political theory of idealism stands and falls with the notion that the state is an institution of an unusual kind. You don't exhaust its characteristics by describing its political structure, the society within which it operates, and the men who run public affairs. Bosanquet compares the state to human mind: it is complex, it challenges and transcends purely physiological descriptions.

Modern mind abhors metaphysical explanations. Anything which is not related and explained directly by the passions and interests of individuals is likely to be rejected as a description of a political phenomenon. Hegel, Rousseau, and hence Bosanquet appear to us, if we share the view stated above, not as political theorists but rather as poets dealing with politics. Yet it is important to keep in mind that most hardheaded and realistic theories of politics have a small core of nontangible values. As stated before, any discussion of politics which goes beyond pure description and ventures into the realm of ethics must have an element of metaphysics or of nonscience in it.

The same is true of Bosanquet's political philosophy. The view of human nature which underlies it has been mentioned before. Man cannot exist in isolation either physically or morally. To know human nature we must not take man in his "trivial" moments of self-indulgence or self-interest. It is here that the liberal theory (and Bosanquet would also add socialism) makes its mistake. Man finds his fulfillment, claims idealism, in getting "outside" himself, in seeking fellowship and unity in a larger context. Man, as a political being, claims political idealism, finds his real "self" in the state. The latter is his "real will" purified of the accidental and capricious. Freedom is thus not only the lack of restraint: it is the capacity of being what we were intended to be, what we yearn to be, and what we can only be as associates in the most complete social institution that has been devised up to date — the state.

It is seen, therefore, that modern idealism in its most representative modern spokesman becomes a type of secular religion. It is worship of the state. As such it is neither anti- nor prodemocratic. It is susceptible of many interpretations. *The Philosophical*

Theory of the State is not a formula; it is a mold which can be filled with varying substances.

It is important to keep in mind the fact that Bosanquet does not attempt to fill in the mold. The claims of writers like L. T. Hobhouse that Bosanquet's *The Philosophical Theory of the State* was in fact a "Prussian theory of the State" miss the point. We can see the confusion more clearly today when we confront the attempts to label any and all theories assigning to the state welfare functions, and so forth, as totalitarian. Bosanquet's theory is distinctive. It transfers the discussion of politics to a different plane than was hitherto used in England. It is an attempt to see the state in itself, somewhat aside from the actions and feelings of human beings who compose it. An attempt like this may be linked to a decline of the buoyant feeling of individualism which infused social thought from the time of Renaissance on. The ideal of human conduct is judged to be too strong for everyday human nature. The church of the Middle Ages reappears in a new guise and the modern state is endowed with powers and significance in consequence of man's fallen status.[66] But the way Bosanquet poses the problem is only a more frank and at the same time more exotic acknowledgment of the dilemma confronting the self-acknowledged liberal writers. Both J. A. Hobson and Hobhouse witness the decline of extreme individualism and go far in meeting a plea for a collectivistic state. But their theory lacks a sure foundation, for this state which is to take an ever increasing role in the direction and control of social and economic life never appears as more than a pale concept. Bosanquet's state may not be much clearer. It leaves many troublesome questions unanswered. But it is at least an ideal. He is unafraid to postulate the thesis that human conduct is affected by an association in a broad national community transcending class and personal interests. He is unafraid to equate self-government with the need for self-discipline and absolute moral values. To an extent those are all words and we may be impatient for some clues to action. We may be equally impatient of a theorist who boldly states that "all sound theory and all good

[66] There is an almost scholastic flavor beneath the Hegelian phraseology in the question Bosanquet asks: "How can a man's real self lie in a great degree outside his normal self, and be something which he only now and then gets hold of distinctly, and never completely?" *Ibid.*, p. 156.

practice are founded on the insight or on the faith." [67] But the
words conceal an enormous change in emphasis from the preceding period of social thought and they conceal the groping for the
new definition of the role of society. It is a great thing to conceive
the true individuality to rest on the basis of a specific service or
contribution which man renders to his society. The common-sense
character of the statement is evident but it is very different from
the famous words in which Adam Smith defined self-interest as
the basis of the individual's contribution to the community. Behind the shift lies a whole century of experience with the liberal
concept of the state on the national and international scale. Behind
it lie various theories begotten during the experiment, with their
programs of class warfare and their analyses of the individual's
helplessness and apathy when confronted with social and political
phenomena.

Bosanquet's theory is an attempt to represent the state as a
positive force in man's life. It is no longer a machine invented to
perform a few necessary and unpleasant tasks. The state is an institution infused with life which lives as a part of each citizen's life,
and which is nourished by the history and moral sentiment of the
community. There can be no rejection or denial of the state by an
individual for in so doing he is also negating a part of his nature
whether he realizes it or not.

What is implied in this relationship is a certain character of the
state which precludes it from being based upon the idea of exploitation. Bosanquet's theory would not allow his state to be a
racist state, or to be based upon exploitation by an economic or
military class. An "imperfect" state would still command most of
the attributes which the state has, but the logical conclusion of his
theory would point toward an institution based upon the idea of
service and *free* association of *all* the citizens. The reason we refused to call Bosanquet's theory more than a mold for a more
definite description of the state is that there are no implications
in the *theory as a whole* that the state should be socialist or nonsocialist in its character or that the type of equality prescribed by
him would still not leave room for an elite. The problem of democracy is tackled but indirectly. It is seen very easily that Bosanquet's

[67] *Ibid.*, p. 155.

main interests lie in defining the nature of the state, and the basis of obligations which the citizen owes to it. It would seem only logical to follow with a prescription of political and economic institutions which the state must embody to fit the description given above. But the task is not even undertaken.

The general statement of the state's role as a "hinderer of hindrances to the best life" would also imply a resolute line of social and economic policy. The principle which makes Bosanquet hedge on social and economic issues may be a sound one: an outright intervention by the state in economic matters has something automatic in it. Insofar as the state undertakes, for example, to cope directly with the problems of individual poverty it may be frustrating the instincts of self-reliance and ambition of the individuals concerned.[68] But there is an academic and unrealistic air about the discussion of the problem so crucial to a theory of the state. There is also a certain unawareness of the fact that the concept of citizenship as postulated by Bosanquet requires certain minimal material standards. The words and the discussion which follows them embody a wise caution and a principle which more enthusiastic believers in state action might well ponder: the improvement of living standards and material security do not per se make a better man or a better citizen and the problem of economic and social reform is largely frustrated if it has only economic ends in view. But by the same token inherent in any given economic and social structure are certain moral consequences. The whole network of economic interrelationships in a modern society contributes not only to the character of political power in the given society, it also contributes to the customs and moral attitudes of the people. The Marxist errs in seeing the economic relationship as the one and only basis for man's behavior and ethics. Bosanquet, on the other hand, may be equally wrong in seeing what might be called the

[68] "Why not, it will be asked, hinder also unemployment by universal employment, over-crowding by universal house building, and immorality by punishing immoral and rewarding moral actions? . . . On every problem the question must recur, 'Is the proposed measure bona fide confined to hindering a hindrance, or is it attempting direct promotion of the common good by force?' . . . We ought, as a rule, when we propose action involving compulsion, to be able to show a definite tendency to growth, or a definite reserve of capacity which is frustrated by a known impediment, the removal of which is a small matter compared to the capacities to be set free." *Ibid.*, pp. 192 and 193.

moral capacity of the individual as something fixed, dependent on the character of the man, and only remotely connected with his social and economic position. And yet the question is crucial to Bosanquet's whole system. Why is the General Will something which sometimes "for the moment, we more or less fail to recognize" though it represents our own ideal of conduct? [69] The answer could conceivably be sought in the differences and peculiarities of social and economic status of various people. In the passage in which Bosanquet quotes, reproachfully, Green's famous criticism of Hegel's definition of the state as a realization of freedom, he exhibits a similar lack of understanding of the social problems underlying the nature of political freedom. [70] Political problems are to him moral problems. Conscious as he is of the onrush of theories explaining man's political behavior in terms of economics and psychology Bosanquet refuses to see social and economic improvement as anything but the question of human will and the inherently moral nature of man. In this lies the source of both the strength and the weaknesses of *The Philosophical Theory of the State*.

THE IDEALIST PHILOSOPHY AS A WHOLE

There is much in idealism which is attractive to a modern man seeking a political philosophy. It offers a clear direction for political endeavor (though its social and economic tenets are less clear), and it avoids at the same time the rigidity of many political creeds. In general there is nothing inherently antidemocratic about the theory. On the contrary some of the idealists, notably Green, minimize the difficulties which exist in the way of transforming a society into a "real" democracy, that is, into a society where a wide diffusion of political power would be accompanied by a substantial measure of equality for all the citizens. Idealism is too apt to treat this question as a simple problem of human volition and accompanies it with the assumption that a theory by being postulated is in a fair way of being achieved.

[69] In the passage from which the quotation is used, Bosanquet speaks of the General Will when it meets us as force (*ibid.*, p. 201), but the statement is true, also, of his general formulation of the relationship between the General Will and the individual will.

[70] *Ibid.*, pp. 288–291.

Hence the inability of the school to see some of the most crucial problems of the modern society.[71]

The important characteristics of a political philosophy are not, however, exhausted by answering the question as to how it suits our prejudices. We must first see a social philosophy as an attempted response to a specific combination of social and historical circumstances. What is the task that the authors of idealism have undertaken?

If we were to translate the language of political philosophy into a statement of problems and anxieties underlying it, it is likely that the case of idealism would stand as follows: "The growth of material civilization and the extension of political rights to the masses have failed to solve any urgent moral and political problems. Not only have such social evils as poverty, war, and class distinctions not been eliminated, but the very progress towards the goals set by the ages of enlightenment and reform has presented and multiplied the old evils in a new and more drastic form. Dynastic wars have given way to imperialist clashes of whole armed nations. The rigid system of economic privilege symbolized by the corporative state has been replaced by the inequalities and sacrifices due to laissez faire. Even the advance towards political and social democracy has been paid for by entrusting political power to the hands of the masses, many of whom are unwilling or unable to exercise it effectively. These results open to question the views of those who maintained that by freeing the individual from as many governmental restraints as possible and by extending political power to the multitude, you could engineer a happier and more prosperous society."

"The error of liberal philosophers" — the idealists would continue — "lies in their conviction that society is merely an intricate machine served by many workmen, who left to themselves without any common purpose can keep the machine going. On the contrary society can be kept going and advancing only through a common ideal, and an institution embodying the ideal. This ideal

[71] Hobhouse notices the point but at the same time renders tribute, inadvertently, to the liberal spirit of idealism: "When Doctor Bosanquet speaks of the institution of a community as the standing interpretation of all the private wills that compose it, he speaks, as though all society were a real working democracy, of the working of society as a whole. This is invariably untrue." Hobhouse, *The Metaphysical Theory of the State*, p. 134.

is the state, since it is the only organization which encompasses all the members of a given society no matter what their differences and origins. The liberals have erred again in treating the state as a sort of policeman — both literally and metaphorically — something quite necessary but hardly praiseworthy and certainly not spiritual in its nature. Yet the state is primarily moral in its character. Since it is the only institution encompassing all, it must essentially represent the interest of all and therefore — since human nature is essentially moral and altruistic — it represents the better, the moral part of human nature.[72] What is needed therefore is a shift of emphasis from individualism to the state. Let us simply enlarge our vision, to allow the state to perform various functions hitherto reserved to the individual. [At least, Green would uphold this point.] With proper precautions the enlargement of the sphere of importance of the state will not result in the detriment of 'true' individualism, for the community is much better equipped to see what an individual through sloth, ignorance, or nearsighted selfishness may overlook. The mere fact of founding a civic religion — the cult of service symbolized by the state — cannot fail to have an elevating effect on public life. For man is not an economic being as the utilitarians pictured him; he is essentially religious in the sense of being a creature with supramaterial cravings. It is the faulty mechanism of society, which exalts material achievements and slights the achievement of service to the common good represented by the state, that leads to class divisions and antagonisms. Rationalism has been abused by the liberal school by linking it with the short-run rationality of economic success, rather than with the long-run rationality of the desire for the security and satisfaction of 'belonging' in a great community."

It is easy to see that Idealism assumes that human problems are essentially of a political nature. The reason for frustration and unhappiness current in a society lies primarily, according to this philosophy, in the faulty concept and structure of the state. To

[72] Inherent in this reasoning is a logical fallacy similar to that of Marx. Marx saw that the only class in the position to abolish capitalism was the proletariat. Hence he assumed that the proletariat was endowed with the qualities and desires to destroy capitalism and establish socialism. Bosanquet and Green see that the state is the only institution which represents all the people rather than a class or a faction, and they are prompt to assume that the state in effect does have a mystical character of impartiality and equal solicitude for all.

Green, for example, the primary cause for the existence of drunkenness is the state's refusal to tackle the problem of temperance, which in turn is due to ignorance of the true nature of the state's functions. The whole argument exudes faith that freedom, the "real freedom," is the supreme answer to human problems. Realize the ideal of the free society, transplant into modern conditions the ideal of the Greek city-state, and you will have solved the most delicate problems of social adjustments.

Yet, it might be argued, political problems are not as important as the idealists and other political philosophers make them out to be. It is clearly naïve to assume that the key solution lies in the field of politics, that the discomfort man experiences within his civilization is due to the faulty political organization of society. The older liberals with their more primitive psychology had, perhaps, a keener insight into the relationship of politics to socially induced frustration. They saw simply political compulsion as the basic and yet unavoidable evil. It is by minimizing political and other forms of social compulsion that they sought to maximize human happiness. The idealists see that by minimizing political compulsion, other forms of social and economic pressure upon the individual can be increased, but they do not indicate the extent and the limits of political compulsion. They decry laissez faire as debasing morally, but except for indicating a few fields where the state might interfere with economic conditions, they leave the whole problem hanging in the air.

The materials of politics are made of human interests and passions. But political idealism does not analyze the passions and interests of the contemporary society. The very existence of a political philosophy implies of course the awareness of certain social tensions. Idealism is too academic as a political philosophy; it treats social problems as if they existed independently of social classes and interests, it treats them as abstract questions of right and wrong. At no point is the question asked: to what interests should an appeal be made, or, what are the most concrete social questions that demand legislative solution. Political philosophy may be excused if it deals in abstractions, but a philosophy which advocates a wider sphere of activity for the state ought to offer a greater variety of concrete proposals.

The appearance of idealism in English political philosophy co-incides with two phenomena, one of political, the other one of economico-social nature.

By the end of the nineteenth century the major political battle has been fought and won by the proponents of democracy — England has achieved a virtual manhood suffrage. The absence of suffrage for women, plural voting, and the existence of the House of Lords were still limiting factors, but political power has been entrusted to the mass of population. The arguments of Disraeli and the misgivings of John Stuart Mill had been left behind, and it became obvious that the future could not bring reversal of the trend. The state still contained remnants of feudalism in its social structure, while the interests of the industrial and commercial class were still in ascendance in its economic policies. How were those to be reconciled with the at least titular predominance of the common man in politics? The problem escaped the attention of political writers of the time. They were content to assume that the traditional current of British political life would go on in its two-party form. The issues which aroused the greatest amount of spec-ulation in the last quarter of the nineteenth century — the problem of Ireland, and the reform of the House of Lords — appear to us, from the perspective of time, rather peripheral.

It might be said that the most obvious fact about the relation-ship of a country's political structure to its social one is that any serious disharmony between the two is liable to produce political and social upheaval. The middle class in France at the time of the Revolution felt itself to be growing in power and influence, and its grievances were due not so much to the autocratic form of the regime as to the obsolete social system which by its existence offered a standing insult to the aspirations of the bourgeoisie. Eng-land in 1900 presented the spectacle of a political democracy and of a class society. The tensions induced by its class structure were to an extent released by political democracy, and by the fact that the dynamics of an industrial country implied a flexible rather than a rigid concept of class. But the danger of disturbance was still implied in the social and political contradiction.

There is no doubt that Green and Bosanquet did not under-stand the nature of the problem. The former viewed the advent of working classes to political responsibility as a task for education. Only minimal changes in the social and economic system were to accompany the educational effort which was to insure that all the classes in England would be composed of "gentlemen." Green and Bosanquet did not see what their follower Lindsay was to perceive, that there is something in the conditions of factory life and wage labor which divides an industrial society and which perhaps cannot be solved by "education," but only by a refashioning of the whole social system.

As long as the industrial supremacy of Great Britain was unchallenged and the system did not appear to be losing its dynamism, the inherent conflict mentioned above did not manifest itself. Socialism as a political movement, as distinguished from a theory, is in a sense the response to scarcity, and in its modern form it is a response to an industrial system losing its dynamism. It was inevitable therefore that as soon as British economy slowed down the dissatisfactions bred by the system, but until then overwhelmed by sheer growth and economic advance, should manifest themselves in the field which became open to the lower classes — politics. A party was to arise that was to take the name and program of a class, rather than of a theory. The dialectic of history, or to use a less metaphysical term, the logic of social development, is better exemplified by the rise and growth of the British Labour Party, than by various "Social-Democratic" parties on the continent which were born out of a theory and always had to try to fit social realities into inflexible frames of a dogma. The Labour Party began as a response to pragmatic needs of the working classes; it coalesced reflecting their feeling and interests, and only then borrowed from the armory of socialist theories. Whether the last achievement, diluted though socialism appears in the party's program, has been of benefit to the movement is at least open to doubt.

It is equally doubtful whether a political party representing the interests and feelings of only a section of the community, born out of a spirit of resentment no matter·how mild, can effectively perform the functions of political leadership. To be sure, almost every political movement is born under such circumstances, but if it acquires power before acquiring a broader political philosophy, it is not likely to make a lasting contribution to the solution of social and political problems. It is unfortunate that idealism missed a closer political tie with the movement which may have needed it most. Bosanquet's political writing was done in the first decade of the twentieth century when the Liberal Party was veering away from the extreme of economic orthodoxy, and after 1906 was actually making first timid steps in the direction of the "welfare state." Yet his work was crowded with abstractions in exclusion of concrete political issues. The opportunity for the type of great influence on political events which political theory can exercise only in a period of social change was missed by idealism.

But the weakness of an "academic" theory of politics does not imply lack of influence. It is rather a certain psychological defect which characterizes the theories engendered and molded in a purely intellectual environment, be they socialist, utilitarian, or idealist. They, for the most part, overlook the state of mind of a man who has to struggle for existence and who has no leisure or temperament for an extended study of less immediate problems. The error may come in two extreme forms: one, that the average man has neither intelligence nor interest in participating in politics; the other, that he is always ready and capable to devote his time to public affairs. The middle ground of concrete politics is illustrated better in the press of the day than in the works of political philosophers. Even within idealism the two theoretical extremes spoken of above are illustrated by Bradley and Green. But the in-between viewpoint, which comes perhaps closest to reality, does not find a spokesman.

Under the conditions of British politics the charge that a political philosophy is too academic does not condemn it to complete lack of influence. Political ideas most often spread from the top, but the peculiarities of British society have made this tendency even stronger. The intellectual atmosphere of a few academic centers in Great Britain has gone far to influence successive generations of statesmen, civil servants, and intellectuals. The impact of idealism in the last quarter of the nineteenth century was greatly felt at that level. It challenged and conquered the dominance of the utilitarian and laissez-faire philosophy, though the latter held sway in public life for some years to come. It was the infusion of the new philosophy which prepared the minds of the people charged with executing and debating policies for the enlarged sphere of state action.[73] Thus the influence of idealism cannot be measured by the relative lack of popular response. Some of its spirit passed into the political atmosphere of the country, and the frame of mind it engendered was conducive to the discussion of pluralism and socialism, which were to dominate English political thought in the first half of the twentieth century.

It might be objected that the facts mentioned above were in themselves undesirable, that a country losing its industrial domination needed a renewal of the capitalist and individualist spirit, instead of theories which in effect prepared the way for a collectivist state. But it is an exaggerated view of the function of political theory to hold it responsible for a major reversal of trend. The weight of objective facts was destroying the old laissez-faire state. The question was: in what direction would the reaction take place? Would it lead to the creation of a Marxist movement of political consequence, or to a more gradual reversal of the political scene, with all the parties and the public opinion adjusting themselves to the change? There is no doubt that the influence of idealism was thrown behind the second alternative. There may be grounds for holding that by failing to make its postulates more concrete idealism failed to inspire more directly a political movement. The decline of the Liberal Party which, paradoxically, started with its triumph in 1906, may have been due to the fact that it was not able to shake off the incubus of extreme nineteenth-century economic liberalism, and the allegiance of the working class was won by a new party narrowly sectional in its interests if not in its ideas or eventual leadership.

A political philosophy is judged among other things by the breadth of interests it displays. When Bosanquet wrote it was already becoming anachronistic to discuss political problems in terms of internal politics only. Yet there is no extensive discussion of international politics either in his work or in that of Green.

Idealism takes over the liberal attitude towards the problems

[73] Among statesmen attracted to idealism were the Conservative Balfour and the Liberal Haldane. The latter, as he recounts in his autobiography, baffled his Army Council when he announced to the generals upon becoming Secretary of War that he had the Hegelian idea of Army!

of international politics. This is rather surprising for we would expect a philosophy exalting the state to tend towards nationalism if not imperialism. The last quarter of the nineteenth century, coincident with Britain's decline from its industrial supremacy, is the only period in modern history when imperialism takes hold on public imagination in Great Britain. Yet the subject of imperial expansion remains relatively untouched by the idealists. Green used to write in rather disapproving tones of Britain's domination of India. Bosanquet for all his talk that state actions cannot be judged by the criteria of private morality rather ignores the subject of foreign relations. What is more important, it does not dawn upon the idealists, and other schools of thought are almost equally oblivious of the fact, that the internal condition of a state is largely determined by its situation in international politics. The spread of liberal ideas in the Europe of the nineteenth century was due not only to purely social and economic causes. It was helped by the fact that the greatest world power of the era was a carrier and representative of those ideas. Yet idealism overlooked, for much worse reasons than liberalism had done, the nexus between domestic and international politics. The error of liberalism lay in its complacency arising from its philosophy of history. War and despotism were by their nature obsolete according to the liberal theory. The spread of free trade was to be the main weapon liberating mankind from these errors. In appraising the position of their own country the liberals were always limited by their eternal distrust of any government. Hence their leaning towards the Little England position, which they preserved anachronistically in the era of great nation-states, and which they bequeathed to the Labour Party. While the idealists abandoned liberal suspicions of state action, in their foreign-policy views they adhered by and large to the liberal tradition. The Empire, the influence of their country in international politics, were for them nuisances since they detracted the state from its proper sphere of action: the sphere of internal improvement, and amelioration of the conditions under which the citizen had to live and exercise his function.

The point is made here to demonstrate that the popular misapprehension of Britain's position and responsibilities in the world which may have contributed to the First World War, and which afterwards culminated in the era of appeasement, was in a sense the legacy of many schools of political thought. Understanding of the phenomena of militant nationalism and of dictatorship was made impossible by theories that made them ghosts of the past, soon to be laid away again in the pages of history. Representative government, material progress, and the absence of widespread military conflicts were made to appear as certain goals of history, instead of being the results of fortuitous circumstances. It was only when the power which had been behind the position of Great Britain was largely gone that the realization seeped into the popular mind that history had not been conquered and that the simple expedients of pacifism were not adequate to deal with the recurrent evils. The omissions of the political theorists appear to us today as their most serious lack of insight. They neglected the most important aspect of the activity of the modern state. Even if we don't attribute exaggerated significance to the warnings of political writers, the results of this neglect — however understandable and sometimes praiseworthy their reasons — were disastrous.

Indirectly, however, taking politics both as internal and as wider phenomena, idealism presents the insight which for all the lack of elaboration is of an overriding value: the state represents the idea that society should go on. The ideal of human collaboration in the widest sphere made effective up to now has value which transcends individual irritations, class conflicts, and even disasters inflicted upon the whole society. The approach to social problems must be, to a large extent, moral in its nature, and the philosophy which reminds us of the point has a lesson for our age.

3

The Fabian Essays

We turn now to a movement, which in its quiet and unassuming way has had a great deal to do with recent political and economic developments in Great Britain. In the light of current developments the *Fabian Essays* still remain alive, and in a sense their message is more relevant today than it was in 1889, though they were not written by men oblivious of their times and looking only to the future. When the chronicler of the Fabian Society reviewed the work of the essayists in 1916 he was at pains to excuse some of their observations and prophecies (for example, "that Liberals would unite with Tories as they have done in Australia and would be confronted with a Socialist Party").[1] Today, after thirty-five years, these criticisms have lost their edge and the *Fabian Essays* appear both relevant and interesting to a student of politics.

The intellectual activity engendered and epitomized in the essays shows how a group of political thinkers can render service to the society they live in and help to mold its institutions. It is by vigorous investigation of contemporary social and economic conditions and a consequent political program, not doctrinaire but common sense, that this service is performed. And, what was most significant about a radical program in the days when socialism was in its militant stage, the essays were permeated by the spirit of

[1] Edward R. Pease, *The History of the Fabian Society*, pp. 92–93.

social reconstruction rather than that of class struggle. The writers evidently believed, and it is a strange belief for a group of young radicals, that while an appeal to the emotions brings speedier political repercussions, the only worth-while results in politics can be brought about by means which are not antithetic to the ends pursued. A patient study of their society and a factual presentation of what appears to be the logic of social development are the aims of the authors of the essays.

In the background lie remarkable changes of economic and political climate in England. After 1880 Benthamite ideas were on the wane. Agricultural crises were accompanied by the dawning realization that Britain's supremacy could not last forever; the specter of serious unemployment made its first appearance. All these phenomena contributed to the intellectual and political ferment of the eighties.[2] Ideas were, as always, affected by the changes in environment. We hear of William Morris, of the Social Democratic Federation, of the beginnings of new unionism. One of the most influential politicians of the time, Joseph Chamberlain (though he was soon to be sidetracked on imperial issues and transformed into a Conservative), conducted a campaign against the "monopoly of land" and for a national system of education and of social services.

The minds of the young people who wrote the *Fabian Essays* were not only registering the impact of social and economic changes that England was undergoing before their eyes. The ideas of John Stuart Mill, of Thomas Hill Green, of Henry George were a potent influence, much better known and real to them than the thought of two obscure German thinkers who within the lifetime of the authors of the essays and in England were constructing a complex system of economic and political theories. Yet as we read the essays we can see that their argument and their flavor are not merely those of dry strictures about the injustice of the existing economic system, about rent, and the extension of franchise which previous writers advocated. There is in the *Fabian Essays* a trace of impatience with the achievements or limitations of the bourgeois society, and a hankering after spiritual satisfaction which,

[2] See Helen Lynd, *England in the Eighteen Eighties*, especially pp. 23–60.

they imply, cannot be found under the conditions of a capitalist society. The writers were a motley crowd, but it is interesting to note that none of them came from the lower classes. There was a heavy sprinkling of literary talent among the early Fabians, and it is possible that the group as a whole viewed capitalism, among other things, as the type of society which produced Undershafts and Ponderevos. The charge of materialism and narrow-mindedness which is often addressed against the capitalist civilization is found not only in political tracts. The same accusation exudes from the great epics of bourgeois life written by Thomas Mann and Galsworthy, and it is found in much of the literature written by authors with widely different political views in any Western country.

It is somewhat surprising that the temperamental dislike of capitalism does not lead the Fabians to advocate abrupt or violent measures. On the contrary it is impossible to exaggerate the cautious and democratic character of socialism which the Fabians advocate. In his essay on the historic basis of socialism, Sidney Webb stresses that socialism is but an inevitable stage in the evolution of democracy. The change must be: (1) democratic, that is, "acceptable to a majority of the people and prepared for in the minds of all"; (2) gradual, causing no dislocation; (3) not regarded as immoral by the mass of the people, and thus not subjectively demoralizing to them; (4) "In this country at any rate constitutional and peaceful." [3]

Nothing can be more democratic and cautious than this precept for reform, and by the same token nothing can be more exasperating to a Marxist. But while pointing out the "inevitability of gradualness" Webb formulates his postulates sharply and uncompromisingly: the receivers of rent and interest are eventually to be abolished as a class through such means as progressive taxation, the differentiation between earned and unearned income, and greatly increased death duties. Step by step with the gradual extinction of many aspects of capitalism is to go the task of educating the masses which implies opening the full benefits of instruction to all citizens and the creation of a Ministry of Education. Leisure is

[3] *Fabian Essays in Socialism*, pp. 31–32.

an essential prerequisite of education. Hence the state is to lead in the reduction of the hours of work, in helping labor to organize, and in improving the system of factory inspection.[4]

The political side of the program is equally concrete. There is still a faint echo of Chartism in the notion of annual parliaments, and the demand for salaries for all public representatives.[5] But there is little in the essays which is revolutionary in the strict sense of the word or not anticipated by the then current progressive ideas in British politics. The plea for an abolition of the House of Lords was then a battle cry of a large segment of the Liberal Party, and its presence in the Fabian program has nothing specifically socialist about it.

Very little in the essays is original from the point of view of political theory but there is a great wealth of economic and social insight. "Capitalism is becoming impersonal and cosmopolitan," writes Clarke,[6] and he notes the emergence of a managerial class, distinct from the owners of capital. The essays stress the theory, today quite commonplace in the literature of evolutionary social-ism but in 1889 quite novel, that the ownership of the means of production is becoming functionless, and that centralization of industry is bound to play into the hands of socialists. The advent of socialism is linked not with the increasing misery of the masses, as Marx would have it, but simply with the factor of technology. Great industries are being "centralized for us by capitalists who thus unconsciously prepare the way for their supercession."[7] The Fabian vision of industrial organization under socialism includes formation of national boards of managers for socialized industries. The boards would be accountable to the nation, just as a private board is accountable to a crowd of shareholders.

Politically the essays display not only moderation, but the type of reasonableness seldom found in a budding socialist group. The existing system, the writers hold, will not collapse once the read-ing public is made to see the moral injustices of capitalism. But the logic of events will show capitalism to be inefficient and ob-

[4] It is characteristic of the authors' background and interests that the reduction in working hours is treated as a corollary of "education."
[5] *Ibid.*, pp. 50–52.
[6] *Ibid.*, p. 80.
[7] *Ibid.*, p. 196

structive. Here is an echo of the Marxist "contradictions" within capitalism which are bound to lead to its destruction.

When it comes to recommending a program of political action the Fabians display the mixture of insight and cautiousness so characteristic of political movements engendered in purely intellectual surroundings. They found political life in Great Britain of their time quite uncongenial to their program. They could not see any difference between the two major parties in their economic programs and assumptions. The Liberal Party according to them had been captured by the manufacturing interest just as the Tory Party had been, though in the latter the paternalistic tradition led occasionally to espousal of workers' interests by particular members (for example, Lord Ashley). In 1889 such an analysis was still correct, though the Liberal Party with Lloyd George was to be different from its Gladstonian model. After this analysis the logical next step was to proclaim the need for a Socialist Party. But the Fabians hold that the time is not propitious for such a party. The prospect of political work as distinguished from intellectual agitation obviously scares them. If you begin by agitation instead of education, you will find yourself competing, on unfair terms, with the demagogues who will raise false issue and propose quack motions of "fair trade," "three acres and a cow," and so forth. You must be sure to prepare the people to act as a true industrial democracy, "To take up the threads when they fall from the weak hands of a useless possessing class. By this means will the class struggle with its greed, hate and waste, be ended." [8]

. It can easily be seen that socialism would have never become a serious political movement in England had it been based exclusively on the Fabian mentality and tactics. But by the same token the useful part played by the ideas and investigations of the Fabians, when they were joined with other social forces, can be ascribed to the modesty and even timidity of the founders, who saw only too well that it would be ridiculous for a handful of intellectuals to aspire to power rather than to influence. At a much later stage in their career some of the original Fabians began to regret their early moderation. In their *Soviet Communism*[9] the Webbs

[8] *Ibid.*, p. 90.
[9] *Soviet Communism—A New Civilisation?* (New York, 1936).

express the feeling that capitalism has proved much tougher than they had expected, and that revolutionary socialism has a great deal of logic to it. But it is more plausible to argue that the "toughness" of capitalism and the rise of fascism are due, among other things, to the revolutionary tactics and attitudes of other branches of socialism. The Fabians don't have to apologize for their aim of "honest purchase" rather than expropriation[10] and for their original purpose of convincing the public opinion as a whole, rather than of indoctrinating a class. Under the conditions of the time it was the only realistic and ultimately fruitful decision they could have taken.

The approach of the Fabians has been often contrasted with that of Marx. It is true that the Fabian movement and British socialism in general have been built upon foundations quite different from those of Marxism. We have here first of all a sturdy spirit of pragmatism, which discounts metaphysics and dialectic and seeks concrete plans and reforms. The violence and the spirit of class struggle of Marxism are absent. As a political theory Fabian socialism has a much weaker dose of materialist determinism than is found in Marxist socialism. Though socialism is envisaged as inevitable due to the evolution of industrial society, the economic factor is not conceived to be the absolute determinant of social and political phenomena. The notion of the "mildness" of the Fabian recipe for socialism is justified only insofar as its method and the tempo proposed for the fulfillment of the program are concerned. When it comes to the ultimate economic objective, the society which would emerge according to the essays would not displease a Marxist.

But a political movement cannot be judged solely on the basis of its aims. Of great importance is the flavor of the philosophy and the spirit in which the proposals are formulated. On this score there is a world of difference between the essays and the standard works of Marx and Engels. There is a strong element of idealism in the essays which, while by no means absent in Marxism, colors the central theme of the program and makes it quite different from most socialist programs. The goal of the reform is to be nothing else but a reform of human nature attendant upon the removal

[10] *Fabian Essays*, p. 180.

of harmful social institutions. Once the insistence upon pecuniary gain is weakened and finally removed the creative abilities of the individual receive a full scope of development. Marxian scholasticism and bitterness are avoided by the writers, but there is just a touch of sentimentality and pathos in the essays which has lingered on in British socialism. The refusal to accept life as a gamble where "many must lose in order that a few may win" leads the writers to undue lyricism when they foresee the society where "the daily bread being certain, the tyranny of pecuniary gain will be broken and life will begin to be used in living and not in struggling for the chance to live." [11] The danger of such effusions is that they weaken the applicability of the theory to concrete situations and they fill political programs with rhetoric and utopias instead of concrete proposals.

Still, the moralizing tone is not the prevailing one in the essays. It serves as an antidote to Social Darwinism, then very much in vogue in England. The link with idealism is tenuous. Sydney Olivier's essay on the "moral" basis of socialism is somewhat reminiscent of Green, but it is in the main a rather clumsy and confused piece of philosophizing, which makes puzzling the author's assertion that his method is that of "unpretentious empiricism." The Fabians took themselves to be the continuers of the tradition of John Stuart Mill and of Jeremy Bentham. Some of their plans of reform bear a direct relationship to Mill's ideas during his last, socialist phase. What does make them in a sense the heir of the utilitarians is a certain disregard for the philosophical issues of politics. There is no thought-out definition of the state, no searching after the concept of law or of sovereignty in the essays. To be sure, just as in the case of the utilitarians, the pragmatism of the school is strongest on the surface, for a definite philosophy of the state does emerge from the concrete proposals. There is more than a superficial similarity between the notion of the General Will and the notion of social change taking place only when it is "acceptable to a majority of the people and prepared for in the minds of all."

It is easy to minimize the importance of the essays. After all their authors did not say much that was new and their insights

[11] *Ibid.*, p. 157.

though valuable were not overwhelming. The importance of the essays lies largely in their flavor, in their amalgam of concrete proposals with a thought-out political basis, and in their combination of an analysis of economic trends with sociological conclusions. Fabian socialism represents radicalism without bitterness. It does not represent an appeal to emotion and, therefore, *by itself* it is politically impotent. And yet it can be and has been of help to a larger and more elemental political movement. The character of the reform advocated by the *Fabian Essays* has gained the support of a large segment of the middle class. In a sense it is not surprising for the essays represent an extension of the rationalist tradition in political argument — the tradition which sprang up and continued with the political ascendancy of the middle class. The Fabian movement has not been the cause of the rise of socialism in England. But it has done a great deal to prepare people's minds for it. It has prepared, especially, the mind of a crucial segment of the society. Popular needs and the consequent pressures and decisions of the electorate contain but half the story of a political change. The other half is contained in the attitudes and beliefs of the individuals who have to frame and execute the details of the reform. It is that important segment of the political body, not limited to the civil service, which has been influenced by Fabian socialism. The Fabian movement acted for a long time as the general and research staff of English socialism, and it has helped to convince, for good or for bad, a large part of the nation that socialism is a refinement and the logical conclusion of democracy.

4

Pluralism

THE GENERAL FORMULATION OF PLURALISM

Margaret Cole's little book on Beatrice Webb makes the complaint which has been a standard one addressed by guild socialists toward their Fabian colleagues: "Webb's conception of economic democracy envisages only collective ownership — state and municipal enterprise — and entirely ignores the functional side, the part that could be played by associations of producers, whether Trade Unions or professional organizations." [1] The complaint represents a "new" political theory of which guild socialism was a part — pluralism.

The Aristotelian truism that man is a social animal rested on the contemporary example of the Greek city-state. It is difficult to compare the latter with our own notions of the state, for the city-state for all its class divisions and the existence of slavery was, at least for a considerable part of its male population, a "men's club" in Professor Zimmern's phrase,[2] or something substantially more than a territory, a bundle of law, and institutions reinforced by a feeling of nationality. The idealist concept of the state, from Rousseau on, has tried to recreate, under modern conditions, the ancient ideal. But the heterogeneity, the size, and other technical attributes of a modern state make even a theoretical reconstruction

[1] Margaret Cole, *Beatrice Webb*, pp. 54–55.
[2] In his *Greek Commonwealth* (Oxford, 1931).

impossible. The city-state was supposedly a community where men's work, worship, and citizenship were blended together. The only modern approximation can be reached through artificial means and force and results in a totalitarian state which again is different from the Greek ideal. The solution from an intellectual point of view is to seek a community smaller and more intimate than the state where man's sociability asserts itself spontaneously. This search is associated with pluralism, which in the years just preceding and following the First World War was a major school of political theory in Great Britain.

It is quite likely that no other school of political thought ever arose in modern times on such purely intellectual pretensions. It is quite striking that the interest expended on pluralism by political writers is quite disproportionate to any political strength the movement achieved, or ever could achieve. Yet the ideas of pluralism spread all over Europe in the first quarter of this century. Even in Russia in the years following the October Revolution pluralism is reflected in the postulates of the "Workers' Opposition." Where is the explanation for this sweep of a theory which was clearly impractical under modern conditions, and which was never formulated with enough clarity to ascribe to it greatness even as an intellectual production?

Pluralism is the last significant attempt in political theory to deny the importance of the state. It is in a sense the legatee of such previous movements of protest as anarchism and laissez-faire individualism. Pluralism as a political theory is largely invented. In other words an attempt is made to set up in theory something to which there is a very small corresponding basis in real life. The aim behind pluralism is well expressed in the words of one of the "inventors": "The mere individual's freedom against omnipotent State may be no better than slavery; more and more it is evident that the real question of freedom in our day is the freedom of smaller unions to live within the whole." [3] The dilemma of the state versus the individual is solved by postulating a third area of social activity. Freedom is seen as the ability to associate and develop in a group of one's own choosing which is not hampered by state regulations.

[3] Figgis, *Churches in the Modern State*, p. 36.

Historically, the foundations of pluralism lie in the works of historians of political thought like Gierke, Maitland, and Figgis. In their attempt to correct the oversimplification of the preceding school of historians, who had conceived the political history of Western nations as the struggle of the individual against the arbitrary state, they went to the other extreme, and saw history as the struggle between the state and various narrower organizations like medieval guilds and churches. Implicit in their views was the judgment that an organization like the church has a life of its own, and is creative both in itself and in relation to its members' lives. The state in its dealing with the church or with any other voluntary group is by contrast a "dead" force of bureaucracy and regulations meddling in something it has no right to disturb. The old dichotomy of the artificial state and naturally free individual is replaced by the one of a free and "natural" group, be it a church or a trade union, and the state which is still artificial since its relationship to its members' personality is remote and based on compulsion. There is a quasi-legalistic flavor to the theory as formulated by Maitland and Figgis. The state "has no right" to meddle in the life of a religious group. This and a certain medievalism implicit in early pluralism should not detract from a valuable insight of the pluralists: freedom becomes concrete only insofar as various organizations are allowed autonomy by the state. An individual is helpless in face of the state, no matter how extensive his rights and how scrupulous their observation, if the state persists in destroying groups and organizations which may compete with it for the loyalty and interests of the individual.

Superficially, the main point of pluralism contains but a truism. Everybody would agree that a state which prohibits or absorbs religious groups, trade and professional organizations, and political parties is not a free state. But if the proposition is pushed further then the question arises how complete is to be the autonomy of various groups. Furthermore, can a state tolerate a group which professes aims quite incompatible with those of the given state? Political life in every democratic country is filled at every moment with concrete cases of conflict, and the state is constantly called upon to adjudicate on the proper limits of activity of a religious or trade organization, just as it is called upon to devise those delicate limits between individual liberty and the obligation of the citizen to his society.

Philosophically and historically, however, the problem of pluralism transcends the commonplace. The very rise of the school denotes a further weakening of atomistic individualism. The notion of separate "interests," of different religions and occupations breeding their own mentality, is an old notion which was seemingly put to rest by the Age of Enlightenment and the rise of liberalism. Man was assumed to be essentially the same no matter what his class or religion. The idea about the special role of religious organizations or professional groups was adjudged to be an obsolete adjunct of the corporative society, a hang-over from the days of feudalism. Now after a lapse of a century the same idea is revived and professed by people who in many other respects hold themselves to be socialists.

The solution to this puzzle must be partly found in the same cause which led to the exaltation of the role of the state — the decline of the belief in simple individualism and rationalism. Those who were not ready to turn to pure collectivism found a compromise solution, they thought, in a revived interest in various groups which have not the compulsory and bureaucratic aspect of the state, but which have, nevertheless, the ideals of service and of common life that give meaning to the individual.

Nobody will deny the contention of Figgis that school and family have a potent influence in one's life, and that the whole network of social groupings and interrelationships "makes" the individual much more than does his membership in the state.[4] Man is not made by society, he is made by various societies to which he belongs. Insofar as the freedom of those societies is curtailed, the real area of man's freedom diminishes. Human freedom, the pluralists argue, is not only the absence of restraint, it is also a function of self-expression. Man is free insofar as he can express his personality and translate into facts his ideas and capacities. The notion is strikingly similar to the idea of "real freedom" embraced by the idealists, with the difference that the locus of self-fulfillment is not the state, but other social groups.

[4] The same point is stressed, for example, by R. M. MacIver; see his *Web of Government* (New York, 1947).

The ideas of pluralism have obviously a great intellectual fascination. They are a compound of the desire for security and the fear of authority which characterize the time of transition. They are a reaction against the utopian view of democracy which proclaimed all men to be not only equal but also alike. But pluralism is pervaded by a spirit of unrealism and wishful thinking. So far as the concrete issues of politics are concerned the mistake of pluralism can be compared to the illusion on which the advocates of disarmament built their activity after the First World War. Instead of tackling the basic causes of international friction and insecurity, they proposed to establish permanent peace through the prohibition of certain forms of warfare and the elimination of certain arms. The pluralists propose likewise to disarm the state, to take away from it certain functions and powers, but they, by and large, overlook the social needs and necessities which underlie those state functions. Pluralism by itself offers a pretty weak argument, and it is only as an adjunct of other social philosophies that it acquires significance in the history of political theory.

The evolution of the political philosophy of Harold Laski offers an interesting example of a gradual departure from pluralism in favor of a more radical and complete answer to social problems. Mr. Laski began his pluralist period in a utilitarian tradition. While talking in that period about various groups within the state and their "wills," he implies strongly that he talks about their interests. The initial problem is: what is to reconcile all these various group interests to prevent our pluralistic society from developing and accentuating all the supposed evils of individualism? The very solution proposed emphasizes the danger: a group endowed with complete autonomy can combine the rapacity and disregard of the common good characteristic of extreme laissez faire with a tyranny over its members comparable to that existing in an authoritarian state. Then appears the temptation to abandon the concept of autonomy of various groups within the state, and to revert to straight collectivism.

Mr. Laski's venture into pluralism leads him to approve of the functional definition of freedom shared by idealism and pluralism. He quotes approvingly the words of Green that "when we speak of freedom as something to be highly prized we mean a positive freedom of doing and enjoying, and that, too, something we do or enjoy in common with others." [5] The implication is that the positive freedom of "doing and enjoying in common" can be realized only in a group smaller than the state. We receive the feeling, however, that Mr. Laski pursues the task of building a pluralist theory with a negative rather than with a positive idea in his mind. He dislikes, at that stage in his career, both individualism and collectivism, but has no genuine devotion to a group-community. He is emphatic that the allegiance to the state should be secondary to the individual's allegiance to society as a whole. Hence we need a system of alternative loyalties which are to be erected to oppose their will to that of the state.[6] The confession that the alternative loyalties are to be "erected" is an acknowledgment that the allegiance to the state is natural and in a different class from our allegiance to other social groups. The very phraseology reveals a certain defeatism in pluralism. The mechanistic approach comes out more clearly in a rather vague statement of what happens when there is a "conflict of wills" between the government and other social organizations. The winner should be the party whose aim is more in harmony with the ends of society as a whole.[7] But this is hardly a description of what happens when there is a conflict between government, and, say, a trade union. The notion that political life is a struggle of various wills for survival is a species of metaphysical Darwinism which tells us very little of what happens in the case of a social conflict. The state as an organization of power is much stronger than any group within it. If we have to have continuous conflicts between its will and "other" wills, there is no doubt which one will emerge victorious. The assumption that the state as such has a will separate from the wills and interests of various groups and communities is a rather surprising one in a pluralist. Mr. Laski would probably explain his "wills" by saying that they emanate from various economic interests. But then we are closer to Mr. Herring's definition of public interest as being a precarious balance established between various interest groups than we are to the original pluralist position.[8]

---

[5] Laski, *Authority in the Modern State*, p. 55.
[6] *Ibid.*, p. 122.
[7] *Ibid.*, p. 65.
[8] E. P. Herring, *Public Administration and the Public Interest* (New York, 1936).

The initial difficulty of all the efforts of pluralists is their studied disregard of the state. Figgis' defense of the spiritual freedom of religious communities and Laski's dislike of centralized authority combined with his plea for social reform lead both of them into a blind alley. The dichotomy between the state and other social groups is as unreasonable as the one between the individual and the state. The society which would fit the dream of the pluralists would be in a state of anarchy, and then it is doubtful whether we would see the period of spontaneous group creativity that the pluralists imagined. The medieval society at which some of the pluralists looked so longingly was a relatively static society. It is also doubtful whether the medieval guild was that ideal setting for human freedom and self-expresion which the romantic imagination of the pluralists makes it out to be. Anyway, the picture of the state as being merely a very loose association of autonomous groups is both unreal and impractical. It may have, as we shall see in the case of guild socialists, some value when it is combined with a definite political philosophy, and with some idea of the institutional framework. Figgis and Laski are both reformers in their separate ways. Figgis pleads for a change in national temper for a realization of the Christian spirit. Laski even in his early stage argues for an economic and social transformation. But it is an undeniable though perhaps unpleasant fact that it is the state which has been the instrument of major social reforms in modern times. It is incongruous to ask for reforms and then to weaken or to abolish the only agency which can perform the task of reform. When Mr. Laski formulates an overall picture of the state and its problems he abandons (in the *Grammar of Politics*) the pure pluralism of his earlier days.[9] Pluralism has had other defenders who developed its ideas more elaborately, but in time they also had to turn towards a more concrete and practical social philosophy.

GUILD SOCIALISM

Socialism as a movement of protest has often been embraced by people close, from the theoretical viewpoint, to anarchism. At

[9] See W. Y. Elliott, *Pragmatic Revolt in Politics*, especially pp. 166–176.

the same time the appeal of socialism to people with strong individualist and anti-authoritarian leanings has always been limited
by the fact that essentially socialism, whether Marxian or non-
Marxian, must argue for centralization of political and economic
authority as the immediate practical steps.

Guild socialism is a product of the marriage of pluralism and
socialism. It replaces the centralizing tendency of socialism by
emphasis upon the decentralization of economic activity. How far
the idea of decentralization of economic activity of independent
producers' cooperatives is compatible with socialism in the first
place is a question which bothers guild socialists, but to which
they do not give a clear answer. One of the advantages claimed
by the advocates of contemporary socialism is its ability to plan
production and consumption and to assure an orderly economic
development. It is obvious that a brand of socialism which gives
up the idea of centralized economy sacrifices a large part of this
claim, and indeed, at first glance, the problems of planning which
would arise under guild socialism look more formidable than those
which a laissez-faire economy would encounter.

The atmosphere of guild socialism is pervaded by all the hopes
and sentiments of which we spoke in discussing the general out-
lines of pluralism. In addition guild socialism is not untouched by
the growing application of psychology to the social sciences. The
ideas of Freud and Jung were now very much in the air. The First
World War seemed to many old-fashioned liberals to deal a decisive blow at the concept of human rationality in its extreme form.
The disorganization which followed the war years was, again, productive of an attempt to steer political discussion towards new
concepts. As in reality so in theory, society seemed to have broken
up into many fragments with their own viewpoints and interests.
The concept of economic man was challenged by the concept of
security-seeking man. The security which was sought was not limited to a modicum of economic well-being. Man was discovered,
or rediscovered, to possess a desire of "belonging," of joining in a
group where he could contribute, and where he could feel shel-
tered from the enormous complexities of society at large. The same
glib explanation was later on applied to illuminate the success of

totalitarian movements. At the time, however, it was advocated to support the theory of a society divided into several large groups, based in the main on their status and occupation.

Guild socialism does not go to the extreme of environmentalism. Its socialism is not of a purely materialistic variety; it has an element of idealism in it.[10] Mr. Cole was emphatic that "human society is neither mechanism nor a machine."[11] But what is it then according to guild socialism? Cole is careful to distinguish between the "community" and society. Community is mainly a mode of feeling of a number of human beings living together under the condition of social life. Society on the other hand is a group of centers of deliberation and planning.

Cole's community is therefore a spiritual concept, while his idea of society is that of a group of economic organizations. Where is the state? That unpleasant concept is at times ignored with a warning that the theories identifying the state with real will are nothing but fraudulent justifications of conservatism.[12] Mr. Cole then is ready to assign some functions to the state. It is to control consumption, but not production![13] This rather bizarre economic postulate is later on expanded into the statement that the state should control incomes and prices! No sooner is the concession made than it is revoked and Mr. Cole becomes extremely dubious whether the state has any claim to survival and allegiance whatsoever.[14]

This is confusion of the worst type. It is, perhaps, the result of the small element of anarchism which found its way into the mixture which became guild socialism. What emerges from Cole's first statement of guild socialism is the typical viewpoint of anarchism: the power of coercion is the root of all evil in social institutions. The concept of the state with its formal paraphernalia

---

[10] "We need not deny or minimize the vast influence of material conditions . . . but we can still believe that the creation of new social forms for old and still more the right direction and utilization of those new social forces which arise out of changing material conditions is a matter which human wills can influence and which indeed depends essentially upon men's active will to take advantage of their opportunities." G. D. H. Cole, *Social Theory*, p. 93.

[11] *Ibid.*, p. 204.

[12] *Ibid.*, p. 193.

[13] *Ibid.*, p. 98.

[14] *Ibid.*, p. 102.

of sovereignty, even with such modifying features as parliamentarianism, is therefore banished. Once coercion is banished the coöperative instinct of man will assert itself. But the locus of social activity is no longer, as with anarchism, a society composed of autonomous individuals, but a society composed, in the first place, of various groups each pursuing its own function. The citizen (if this not be an improper name) may belong to several groups. The abolition of exploitation and of coercion assures a gradual evanescence of the last traces of the state. This view is held to be not a utopia, but a scientific exposition of what is actually happening in our society.

More than most philosophies of government guild socialism goes into the mechanics of government. The object of the movement is an achievement of democracy. But democracy is conceived not only as a political system but also as a way of life. "Democracy is only real when it is conceived in terms of function and purpose." [15] Consequent upon this declaration is a different system of representation than the one employed even under most democratic constitutions. People cannot be represented merely as an aggregation of individuals nor can their will be represented by the will of an elected representative. What can be represented is the part of their personality, the purpose which has gone into an organization of which they are active members. Any true representation must be functional. Human personalities with all their infinite meanings and variations can never be counted like telephone poles. It is the crystallized aspect of human personality — man's religious or professional affiliation — which is a significant datum for politics. It is simple then to say that every man should have as many votes as he has interest functions.[16] The principle of plural voting has a remote relationship to Aristotle's "distributive equality" and is in a striking contrast to the prevailing democratic theory. It does not occur to guild socialists that any practical attempt to realize their own version of "plural voting" might lead to absurd results. The very fact that the principle is advocated by a socialist movement is a testimony to the breakdown of the rationalist concept of democracy which underlay the "one man-one vote" slogan.

[15] Cole, *Guild Socialism Restated,* p. 31.
[16] Cole, *Social Theory,* p. 115.

The machinery of the state is to guild socialism of secondary importance. What is supreme in their mind is the need for industrial democracy. The latter envisages a clearly syndicalist society as the only type of society able to call out the creative instinct in the mass of men. Capitalism has suppressed this instinct for a long time, and it may take a violent revolution to sweep away the debris of the old system. The plea for syndicalism is thus linked with an undertone of Marxism. The main philosophy of guild socialism has much in common with the thought of many independent thinkers all the way from Saint-Simon to Veblen but what holds the movement together is an undeniable link with socialism.

The guild society of the future is envisaged as a loose confederation of producers' unions. Leaders of the guilds are to be elected by the workers and the whole intricate system is to be topped by the Industrial Guilds Congress. The function of defending the consumers' interests is assigned to a special organization of their own.

It is an irony of history that the only modern state which adopted a formal structure similar to the one described above was Fascist Italy. The whole structure is proposed by its academic sponsor with a great deal of naïveté not only concerning the facts of politics, but also those of industrial unionism. The hateful concept of the state steals back into the picture at every step. Consider the Commune which is to be composed of the representatives of various functional bodies. It is professedly a coördinating not an administrative body, but what are its duties? They are: (1) to allocate national resources and to regulate incomes and prices; (2) to adjudge differences between the guilds; (3) to demarcate the spheres of activity of the functional bodies; (4) to conduct foreign relations; (5) to have coercive functions.[17] What more could the most thoroughgoing collectivist desire?

Yet though the powers granted to the state are extensive they are given grudgingly, and with a clear intent that the state — the Commune — should be an artificial, purely utilitarian device. How is the Commune's authority going to be respected by various functional groups when it is to arbitrate between their claims? The

[17] Cole, *Guild Socialism Restated,* p. 140.

notion of public interest as embodied in the state is often abused, but it cannot be replaced by a vacuum.[18]

S. G. Hobson, whose writings have been rather neglected by students of the movement, faces the problem of the state in a different vein. The state becomes the embodiment for him of "the citizen will" which it can impose upon any recalcitrant individual or section of the community.[19] The phraseology of Hobson might be that of Hegel or Bosanquet. The state expresses the spirit of the community, it expresses "the abiding truths" of the national and international situation, and in general stands against selfish interests of particular segments of the community.[20] Where is the source of Hobson's guild socialism when his language stems directly from the idealist tradition? He himself attributes it to his preoccupation with "craftsmanship" and the recognition that under capitalist conditions the majority of people cannot do more than earn their living. Hence the desire to abolish "wagery" and to replace it by workers' monopoly of their labor, which will change their attitude towards work.[21]

Hobson's formulation of guild socialism does not therefore eliminate the state. He is in agreement with the idea that industrial labor has to be turned from being an occupation into something approaching a vocation. There is an element of positive worth in his idea, however farfetched. It may be that it is the monotony and routine in most industrial work, more than anything else, that produces class struggle. Guild socialism takes the point of view that even a relatively high standard of income and security for the workers will not suffice in itself, if the workers are not conscious of being more than just cogs in a big machine. They emphasize the evil of capitalism from the angle of "wagery" rather than that of exploitation. There is some similarity between the guild socialists and Thorstein Veblen on this point. It is interest-

[18] For a detailed criticism of Cole's concepts, see Elliott, *Pragmatic Revolt in Politics*, chap. vi.

[19] S. G. Hobson, *National Guilds and the State*, p. 106.

[20] *Ibid.*, p. 143.

[21] In one of his earlier books Mr. Cole toyed with the Rousseauistic conception of the state, and proclaimed syndicalism as the means of freeing the state from less important tasks. He approached Hobson's concepts and spoke of that "elusive but fundamental reality which he (Rousseau) named the General Will" (*The World of Labour*, p. 28). But eventually Cole went much further in his syndicalism.

ing to notice in passing that the most recent Marxist pronounce-
ments on the subject also tend to attack capitalism for its choking
effect on the creative element of productive labor. Guild socialism
when it does not go to the ridiculous extreme of ignoring or "abolishing" the state has a useful insight in seeing the conditions and
atmosphere surrounding industrial labor as one of the most important facts in our social system. The insight is valuable especially
since it was completely disregarded by the old school of liberalism,
and has been even neglected by Marxism because of its emphasis
on "exploitation." There is also no doubt that in their plans for a
new society Hobson and Cole are motivated by a genuine feeling
for democracy, however impractical the proposed details may be.
The proposal for an effective association of all the people connected with an industrial undertaking, from the manager to the
porter, is undoubtedly of some value. We may not give everybody
an equal voice in determining the policy of a given enterprise, but
there is room in smaller units for the type of equality and exchange
of information which the democratic theory assumes about our
society as a whole. In many questions affecting national policy
the average citizen must remain an observer since he has no knowledge or leisure to affect the decision, but everybody has the
power to contribute something within his own, narrower sphere.
It is in elucidating this most commonplace idea that lies the greatest service of guild socialism.

It would be mistaken, though, to assume that guild socialism
is completely free of revolutionary undertones. Hobson's proposals
show him to be not overly concerned with constitutionalism. The
new society according to him will spring up through extralegal
methods — trade unions arrogating to themselves more and more
power. When it comes to compensating the owners for their industrial property Hobson does not stop very short of expropriation.
His tone is that of impatience with the settled forms of political
life. Curiously enough Hobson envisages his plan as a defense of
Western civilization against Bolshevism. There is an element of
mysticism in all this. Materialism is denounced in violent terms,
and one of the reasons advanced in favor of freeing the state from
its economic tasks is that it should confine its activity to "spiritual"
matters. Hobson, unlike other guild socialists, is not afraid of na-

tionalism. The state as the carrier of purpose should instill democracy in every sphere of national life. On one very concrete and important issue of political life Hobson takes a definite stand. Civil servants owe their allegiance to the state (he would include the educational guild among the civil servants), and the state should protect them only in the conditions of their employment.

Guild socialism has produced many writers but G. D. H. Cole and S. G. Hobson are undoubtedly the most important ones in the English language. A R. Orage is close to Hobson in the flavor of his philosophy and in his conclusion. Arthur J. Penty illustrates the frankly obscurantist side of the movement. He would abolish industrialism, curtail industrialism, curtail international trade, and he looks fondly upon the Middle Ages with their notions of the "just price," of "private property for common use," and so forth.[22]

The preoccupation with medieval notions is perhaps one of the most curious things attending guild socialism. The name of the movement is in itself characteristic: that an intellectual movement which calls itself socialist should adhere to medievalism is, perhaps, a good indication how history is used and abused for the sake of political fancy. What appeals to a reactionary when he envisages the Middle Ages (as if the period were a monolithic whole) is their emphasis on status and class division. By the same token the guild socialist sees in the period the absence of the state in the modern sense of the word and the emphasis on other than material elements of human nature. Both views, it is hardly necessary to say, contain gross oversimplifications. The nostalgic feeling bred by the dislike of industrial civilization is closely akin to the literary tradition in English literature which stretches over a long period of time including such names as Carlyle and Ruskin, and Belloc, Chesterton and Aldous Huxley in our own day. It is difficult to build a political theory from a purely negative element. Guild socialism was constructed by people who were quite sure of what they did not like, but who were not equally sure of what they wanted. The movement lacks the historic logic of collectivism, and it does not share in the moral appeal of individualism.

Guild socialism, however, is not to be dismissed as a movement without significance. The focus of political activity recommended

[22] See Arthur J. Penty, *Old Worlds for New* and *Guilds, Trade, and Agriculture*.

by it is a very vital *secondary* focus of our political life. The
struggle between collectivism and individualism neglects the intermediate area of associations and organizations. The power and
complexity of the modern state, against which guild socialism
registers a helpless protest, can be tempered by a more positive
approach to the area of activity found in various smaller groups.
From an ideal point of view those groups can be valuable schools
of citizenship and democracy. A variety of recent studies[23] attribute the rise of fascism to the sense of isolation the individual experiences in modern society. Likewise our philosophers of business
have stumbled upon similar explanations of industrial conflicts.
Without attempting a closer analysis of such claims it is quite
reasonable that they should contain at least a grain of truth. Western political tradition is still the heir to the early liberal notion
that man is a rational, autonomous, and individualistic being and
that he needs society, as a whole, only for his "artificial" needs.
The philosophy which proclaims that it is a vital necessity to the
individual to be accepted within an intimate group or association
has its value insofar as it corrects the earlier overemphasis on individualism.

The more specific points of guild socialism are more difficult
to accept. The notion that a man's political or trade affiliation
should supersede his citizenship is clearly unrealistic. The rise of
the modern state has witnessed the ever recurring effort to delimit
the respective spheres of allegiance. If guild socialism has as its
main objective security, both material and psychological, then the
abolition of the state (if it were possible) would not enhance but
destroy the security of the individual. It is becoming increasingly
obvious that even a national state may not be a sufficiently big
unit to provide the feeling of security, that is, in the economic
sense of the word. A loosely knit community in which various
organized interest groups would battle each other would hardly
be an improvement on modern democratic state. There is little
evidence that the abolition of capitalism would enable various
interest groups to coöperate peacefully without the interposition
of the state. The harmony-of-interests theory when applied to

[23] E.g., Erich Fromm's *Escape from Freedom* (New York, 1941).

professional and trade organizations is less and not more convincing than when it was used to justify laissez faire.

There is also no doubt that the aesthetic protest of guild socialism is in reality a Romantic hang-over. A political theory is today obsolete if it cannot absorb the facts of industrial civilization. The yardstick of success applied today to working political philosophies is increasingly made of the facts of production and the standard of living. As an opponent of capitalism, guild socialism cannot compete with socialism in the proper sense of the word. A philosophy of politics cannot succeed if it sets itself against the ruling passions and interests of the age. Guild socialism by-passes the question of economic expansion, and it almost ignores the problem of nationalism. It is those omissions, rather than the theoretical faults and contradictions, that have been most fatal to the success of the movement.

5

The State and
Neo-Idealism

THE CHALLENGE OF MARXISM

Socialism is the prevailing political philosophy of our age. This in itself does not assure its victory nor warrant its ultimate acceptance. The ascendancy of eighteenth-century rationalism did not result in the kind of state the Enlightenment envisaged, and nineteenth-century liberalism for all its political and intellectual successes in the West did not exorcise the evils of dictatorship and militant nationalism in the world. Socialism is in very much of the same position today; it presents a confluence of theory and objective facts which makes it impossible to ignore. Nonsocialist writers on politics and economics are to a large extent antisocialist. It is hard to analyze any social phenomenon without having in mind the most buoyant political theory of our age.

What are the reasons for the dominance of the political scene by socialism? The term admits of many definitions. Like other dogmas it is split up into many factions. Like other ways of arranging social and economic systems it varies depending upon circumstances and specific applications. It would be presumptuous here to go into details of its many variations, or into the history of the idea. But Marxism requires comment from anybody who tries to describe a tendency in contemporary political thought.

The theories of idealism, of Fabian socialism, and of guild socialism possess many points of resemblance to Marxism. Idealism goes far in emphasizing the role of the state and in deprecating the "excesses" of individualism. Guild socialism shares perhaps most closely with Marxism the analysis of the capitalist state: this state is an organ of exploitation which by the weight of its institutions saps the productive and creative instinct of men. The *Fabian Essays* give a more prosaic version of the Marxist dialectic: the inevitable tendency of history is towards greater industrial centralization culminating in the ownership of the means of production by the state. These movements, which except for guild socialism have not been influenced directly by Marxism, point to a great variety of objective changes in social structure and in intellectual atmosphere which happened to coincide with the formulation of many Marxist postulates.

First among them is the growing role and importance of the state. The growing size and intricacy of the social structure has doomed Spencerian individualism. The traditional antistatist theories lived in the world of small economic units, when the significance of individual endeavor was much greater than it could possibly be today under any political or economic system. The individual as seen by old-fashioned liberalism was an idealized member of the middle class, rational, suspicious of doctrines and slogans appealing to the emotions, and able to regulate his behavior without the interference of the government. Equally important from the point of view of the theory which exalted individualism and minimized the state was the assumption that as mankind should progress armed conflicts and imperialism would cease. Free trade was to be in international relations what representative government was in the domestic politics of Great Britain: a brake upon political emotions and class (national) conflicts, the best way as well as the best education in solving the clashes of power and interest. What has damaged liberalism most has been the failure of its prophecies in the international sphere. The state has grown in importance not only because of purely mechanical reasons, but also because the twentieth century has been an almost uninterrupted period of "emergency" for much of the civilized world with the consequent tendency towards concentration of political power.

It is interesting to note that more than any triumph of philosophy it has been the logical sequence of history that has favored socialism. Democracy remained for a long time a political philosophy without a practical component, and it was the *levée en masse* and the new concept of war as embracing whole nations which demonstrated the practicability of democracy. Similarly, modern warfare with its paraphernalia of planning, rationing of supplies, and commandeering of resources has provided a better preview of a socialist state than the one imagined by the theoreticians, and has conditioned people's minds to many aspects of socialism.

But the success of socialism, and especially of Marxism, cannot be explained merely as a consequence of a fortuitous arrangement of events. Marxism possesses a great tactical advantage over democratic liberalism insofar as the latter has been secular and unemotional. The success of what is normally conceived to be the pattern of democratic government has been its ability to harness the process of revolution to that of orderly government. The machinery of political parties and of the judicial process serves to protect the individual against the state, and at the same time to unload political grievances without violence and without injuring the continuity of the state. One of the aims of any concept of government is the ability to preserve the continuity of its political system even in the face of natural or economic disasters. The machinery of a liberal state has, in accordance with the liberal dogma, allowed the creation and organization of political and social grievances. What has prevented these pressures from exploding and destroying the very fabric of the democratic state has been the device of political party which enables an orderly alteration in government of varying political philosophies. But in addition, the factor stabilizing the democratic government has been the dynamic economic development of the West. The rising standard of living has minimized the importance of protest and revolt which the liberal democratic state cannot help generating by its very existence. Periods of emergency and the decline of free trade (in the broader sense of the word) are the great threats to the dynamic of capitalism, rather than being, as Marxism tries to convince us for obvious psychological reasons, the very symptoms and consequences of declining capitalism.

The present situation therefore confronts a democratic state — let us say Great Britain — with crucial economic-political dilemma. It must either recover the pace of economic progress under world conditions which are clearly antithetic to the original liberal assumptions, or it must contain by its political system the social unrest which is let loose by the loss of economic dynamism. The same difficulty does not confront socialism in the same degree. Socialism, to be sure, is also founded upon a promise of a higher standard of living for all, but it also contains a variety of social and moral postulates which can become emotionally satisfying goals, and which may prevent it from being judged, at least by its partisans, purely on the basis of its economic achievement. The achievement of "social justice," of "equality" are the arguments, and it is not suggested they may not be valid arguments, which can cover up other weaknesses of a regime. Due to the shifted focus of political power such achievements appear more persuasive than purely political achievements of a liberal state. Nondemocratic socialism has a still greater "advantage": the achievement of its social objectives will become an almost metaphysical goal, and its imperfections insofar as the conditions of living and liberty of its citizens are concerned recede still farther as the bases of its self-criticism.[1]

Socialism, therefore, as an ideology competing for power (whether this ideology is actually called socialism or not) in a democratic society has definite tactical advantages over its opponents. In addition various theories connected with socialism, but not necessarily with its central thesis, contain valuable insights into social development, and also important moral truths. There is a very great temptation for a political writer of a nonsocialist persuasion who rejects Marxism to absorb many elements of that variety of socialism. No political ideology ever

[1] The proponents of both socialism and communism claim, of course, that their systems do lead to a higher standard of living. What is claimed here is only that a failure of those systems on the count of *immediate* improvement of the conditions of living of the citizen is not taken as seriously either by their partisans or their enemies as is a similar failure on the part of capitalism in a democratic state.

triumphs in a pure form; it is bent and conditioned not only by the force of circumstances but also by other and competing political philosophies. It is therefore quite likely that the modern state will eventually contain many elements of socialism, though it will not necessarily be socialist. The point is to what an extent will Marxism color these socialistic features. Schemes of social security, of government control over economy, and so forth are common features of all the civilized states today. Yet by themselves they do not make a state socialist, and they are not the decisive features of a Marxian state.

The revival of idealism in contemporary England is largely the work of A. D. Lindsay. But Lindsay, himself a member of the Labour Party, tries to endow his neo-idealism with a concrete political program. In reading his works one is struck by the obvious attempt to synthesize various strains of thought into a philosophy which would be more concrete and up to date than the philosophy of Green and Bosanquet, and which would go at the same time beyond party programs into a reasoned philosophy of democracy with strong socialist undertones.

Lindsay tries his hand, for example, at a reinterpretation of Marxism.[2] Marxism, unlike socialism as a whole, is a definite political philosophy rather than a general approach to social problems. Like other political philosophies it has various strains in it and even inconsistencies, but it has its main points of emphasis well set forth by its founders and they cannot be modified without doing violence to the doctrine. The attempt to swerve Marxism towards idealism, which by its very nature must reject the emphasis on economic determinism and class warfare, is liable to be at least a partial failure. Yet this is exactly what Lindsay tries to do.

Marxian determinism is strongly diluted in Lindsay's critique: "Economic determinism then, according to Marx, is not represented as the last word about the whole of man's nature, but as a fact to be recognized and overcome."[3] This is a rather surprising statement from a historian of political thought. To be sure, man is eventually to be freed, in the communist utopia, of economic

[2] Lindsay, *Karl Marx's Capital, An Introductory Essay.*
[3] *Ibid.*, p. 36.

determinism. If from primitive times until today the conditions of production have determined social structures and cultures, if the dominance of the economic element is not to be eliminated until the final dissolution of the state, until the "state of nature" has been recreated — to be sure, under vastly different technological conditions — then how is economic determinism to be overcome under the actual conditions of politics? The meaning of Marxism is still more obscured when we read that Marx taught that "Freedom cannot be achieved by a political state which leaves economic relationships uncontrolled by a common purpose . . . Till they are so controlled, economic relations are a blind force and until that blind force is mastered it is useless to talk of political freedom." [4] Economic relations, according to Marx, are not a "blind force." They follow a pattern laid out by his theory. The notion of a common purpose in the state, before capitalism has been eliminated, and not counting momentary issues which may unite the workers and the bourgeoisie (for example, a common front against the remnants of feudalism, or for national liberation), is alien to Marx.

Lindsay's treatment of Marx is apt, therefore, to be somewhat misleading. This does not negate the fact that he does analyze some parts of Marxism with brilliant insight.[5] But Marx emerges, on the whole, from Lindsay's essay curiously similar to Green. The idea behind such an interpretation of Marxism is, undoubtedly, a pious hope not only that Marx can be brought into the fold of great social reformers, but also that there are elements in his theory which are not antagonistic to the evolutionary and constitutional socialism which Lindsay himself embraces. The vague and deeply buried hints of idealism in Marxism are presented as constituting its core. Even the deterministic tenor of the philosophy is deëmphasized, for we are to assume that Marxism teaches that only "Where human will abdicates material conditions are supreme." [6]

---

[4] *Ibid.*, p. 37.

[5] E.g., the statement (*ibid.*, p. 114) that the labor theory of value was for Marx what natural right theories had been for Rousseau: a symbolic expression of moral truth rather than a purely scientific statement of facts. Lindsay sees both theories as morally inspired myths.

[6] *Ibid.*, p. 42.

It is interesting to draw upon another critic of Marxism in this connection. Professor Schumpeter in his book strongly denies that Marxism has any moral connotations (except as a species of religious fanaticism). The success and the imminent victory of socialism are subtly ascribed to the degeneration of the ruling capitalist elite and to the perpetual problem of human irrationality.[7] Victorious socialism is not likely to be democratic, and there is a hint in the book that the growth of socialism is an attendant feature of the decline of our civilization.

Lindsay's presentation of Marxism fits in with his own version of socialism. He aims to take the edge off the Marxist view of society, to harness it to the task of reform rather than that of revolution, and to make its partisans abandon those parts of the program which smack of pure violence, and which defy peaceful transformation. By itself, Lindsay implies, control of economic forces and the redistribution of wealth amount to very little. They are supremely important insofar as they tend to make the state a true democracy, the term comprehending all of the socialists' postulates and much more. Capitalism and its theoretical backbone — laissez faire and old liberalism — do not get a hearing before Lindsay. The economic system which has dominated the West for so long is dismissed abruptly. It is only fair to say that the problem of economic efficiency interests Lindsay very little in itself. If he were to formulate an indictment against capitalism it would be as strong in times of prosperity as in times of depression. He could repeat with Tawney that

poverty is a symptom and consequence of a social disorder, while the disorder itself is something at once more fundamental and more incorrigible, and that the quality in their social life which causes it to demoralize a few by excessive riches is also the quality which causes it to demoralize many by excessive poverty.[8]

It is interesting to note how often arguments against capitalism bear this scholastic flavor. The question why capitalism as such was never popular in intellectual circles may be a sociological one: the system deprecates the importance of the intellectual class,

---

[7] See Schumpeter, *Capitalism, Socialism and Democracy*, especially chaps. vi and xviii.

[8] R. H. Tawney, *The Acquisitive Society*, p. 5.

and it has the tendency to evaluate achievement in pragmatic businesslike terms. The urge of the intellectual to change the values of the society in which he lives is, of course, not always connected with the way his society is treating him. The urge is often connected with his increased sensitivity and speculative tendencies. The intellectual who, like Lindsay, finds himself drawn towards Marxism and yet prefers the middle way is an ideological descendant of John Stuart Mill. Mill, who in his life ranged from pure utilitarianism to a variety of socialism, could be bitter about the system his friends helped to create. It was he who wrote that if the only alternative to communism (meaning socialization of land and the means of production) were the then existing system (of unrestrained capitalism) then all the difficulties, real and imaginary, would appear as flimsy.[9] The same feeling, it is possible to assume, pervades many of today's radicals, but it is coupled with a belief that there is another alternative.

The influence of Marxism is very pervasive since every political and social writer of today reacts to it one way or another. Lindsay absorbs a version of Marxism into his system. He at the same time rejects Marxist conclusions and substitutes idealism for class war. But idealism largely precludes the type of social analysis which Marxism demands. Many of the critics of Marxism reject Marxist economics and conclusions while adopting Marx's view of society. One could name Pareto, Sombart, and Schumpeter among others. They define socialism, and there is a mixture of condescension and envy in their definitions, as a new religious faith. In a sense, Marxism is a faith; it has a mythology of its own and a prophetic element which makes it more than a social philosophy. In comparison with the religious element of Marxism, idealism lacks the prophetic ingredient; it looks at history not in a deterministic way, and its roots and ideology are largely in the Christian tradition.

The challenge of Marxism is the one that any competing political philosophy must meet. It may be paradoxical that this philosophy, one branch of which is represented by one of the most bureaucratic and dictatorial regimes in the world, should evoke so many examples of individual fanaticism and idealism.

[9] Mill, *Principles of Political Economy,* p. 208.

There are historians who, like Mr. Laski, see in the devotees of Marxism, whether of the Communist or non-Communist variety, evidence of the same spirit which motivated the partisans of the Puritan and of the French revolutions. It is true that in order to appreciate the strength of radical socialism, and here British socialism does not qualify for it has operated in a more fluid and free society, one must see it against the background of countless injustices, frustrations, and irritations which spread throughout a whole social system. To those who embrace Marxism for personal reasons, the decision does not come as the result of Marxist economics or view of history, but as something approaching religious conversion. There are novels in which the sense of mission which Marxism attributes to itself is better dramatized than in its theoretical works. One can think, for instance, of Malraux's *Man's Fate* and then reflect that there are no contemporary novels which attempt to dramatize liberalism or the "middle road." Socialism, and especially Marxist socialism, is today surrounded by a species of romanticism which usually surrounds revolutionary movements. But, of course, once it becomes a ruling system it loses the attraction of revolt and acquires many of the drab characteristics which every system of laws and administration must possess. But the lesson of its emotional appeal is the one which non-Marxist philosophies cannot ignore. The struggle of rival ideologies will be resolved largely on the basis of social and economic effectiveness, but it is far from unimportant which ideology can stir up human imagination and almost religious devotion.

TWO APPROACHES TO SOCIALISM

Marxism is distinguished from other brands of socialism by its insistence upon dialectic, and the linking of its postulates to a rigorous theory of economics, the most important part of which is the so-called labor theory of value. At the same time contemporary socialists, especially in Anglo-Saxon countries, do not stress dialectic, considering it a Hegelian encumbrance upon the Marxian system.[10] What is retained is a general feeling of the

[10] The tendency to disparage the importance of Hegelian elements in Marxism comes out, for example, in Paul Sweezy's popular treatment, *Socialism* (New York, 1949), pp. 118-119.

inevitability of socialism without dressing it in metaphysical formulas.

The labor theory of value and its corollaries in original Marxism have been, from the point of view of non-Marxists, completely undermined. What remains as a fighting postulate of Marxism are various propositions based upon the theory and the practical demand that "surplus value" should be taken away from the exploiters and transferred to the community at large.

It will be seen, therefore, that the two key concepts of original Marxism have been weakened even in the minds of its believers and theoreticians. When we speak of Marxism as an ideology we must refer to a general viewpoint and to a philosophy which serves as a basis both for analysis of existing institutions and for social action. From this perspective Marxism is characterized generally as a utilitarian and materialistic creed. It bases its analyses upon an examination of property relationships in a given society, especially but not exclusively upon the mode of production. As theory its standard of values is a purely utilitarian one. (It is only as a movement fighting for power that it becomes endowed with the pseudoreligious characteristics of which we spoke.) Indeed, if we take only the standard of values of Marxism, and forget its social and historical analysis (though even there we find points of resemblance), it fits perfectly with the utilitarianism of Jeremy Bentham.

There have been, ever since men became interested in political theory, socialist theories oriented towards a nonutilitarian scale of values. The most primitive and the most persistent argument for socialism has been a plea for equality, and it is, indeed, possible to consider all theories of socialism as refinements of the original argument. The argument for equality may be given a peculiar twist as in the case of Plato's "guardians," where material inequality is asserted to be a corrupting influence and hence to be stunting the higher faculties of men. There is also an argument akin to Plato's and yet different from it, in which socialism is asserted to be a necessary adjunct of an idealistic conception of the community. The argument might be summarized as follows: "The ideal of human existence can be found in the life of an integrated community, the members of which are aware of

their mutual obligations and duties. Such a community by definition excludes the possibility of great inequalities of wealth and
status. While particular inequalities in income and so forth are
not important and can be tolerated, the state cannot allow any
vested interests and it must be able to regulate national economy
and curtail the claims of private property whenever the interest of
the community demands it."

This definition of a brand of non-Marxist socialism may be
criticized as hardly being socialism, and as being applicable,
in large part, to a mainly capitalist state like the United States.
Nevertheless, a purely materialistic outlook and the insistence
upon the phenomenon of class war are not the only distinguishing
marks of socialism, and one can arrive at socialism from an idealistic point of departure. The seeds of this type of socialism were
observed in the case of Green. They are further developed by
Lindsay.

The philosophical basis of Lindsay's views is revealed in his
debate with Laski before the Aristotelian Society. The subject
of the debate may appear irrelevant to socialism: it is an evaluation of Bosanquet's General Will. Yet the deeper philosophical
analysis which underlies the socialism of both men comes out
very well. It is curious that two men, both of whom have belonged
to the Labour Party and have considered themselves socialists,
should show themselves completely unable to speak a common
language. As a contrast in personalities the debate is also of some
interest. It shows two approaches to politics. One, Lindsay's,
emphasizes the philosophical and moral problem lying behind
politics; the other, Laski's, views politics from the angle of action,
and displays some impatience with the injection of philosophy
into something which is primarily a pragmatic issue.

With Lindsay we go back to Rousseau's General Will. He
rejects the organic interpretation of the General Will. Society
is not a person nor has it a will as a whole. What Rousseau attempted to do with his concept was to set off the contrast within
the individual between his moral and his "selfish" wills. The
moral will has to be of a general character, and thus it resembles
Kant's "categorical imperative." [11] The claim for freedom implies

[11] *Proceedings of the Aristotelian Society,* Suppl., VIII (London, 1928), 37.

therefore a recognition of the rules which guarantee freedom to others.

The discussion may appear not to be related to socialism, but within it are certain formulations of a possible basis of non-Marxist socialism. Man, according to Rousseau, and Lindsay goes along with him, is not a mere creature of material circumstances. As Plato said, the individual is motivated by two sets of instincts. First, there is the selfish, acquisitive instinct corresponding to purely environmental forces acting upon the individual. In the second place there is a "general," altruistic instinct which enables men to be "really" happy in a close association, and consequently implies the desire for the type of society in which most people could achieve the maximum amount of freedom. The way is open to non-Marxist socialism, in which state control of economy and a modicum of economic equality is asserted to be necessary to liberate the social instinct of men.

Lindsay gives an individualistic twist to Rousseau's General Will. The concept is assumed not to be a preliminary to building up a Leviathan-like state, but rather to illustrate the double nature of man and his desire to be freed from the slavery of purely selfish instincts in favor of a broader perspective embodied in the welfare of the whole community. One can see the indebtedness to Green's tortuous attempt to break down the artificial and commonplace contrast of the individual versus the state. In its place we have a commonplace but somewhat complacent assertion that what is best in the individual is social in its nature; and that the best society is the one which stimulates and develops human personality.

In order to bridge the gap between the individual and the state with something more than a phrase Lindsay, whose approach is throughout eclectic, reaches into pluralism. He thinks of three kinds of groups or associations which can mediate, so to speak, between the individual and the state. We have first, for example, purely economic associations. Their purpose is to secure more efficiently what men strive for in their individual capacity. There are other groups existing for the achievement of a limited objective specified in their constitution. Finally we have organizations which have life of their own, to whom justice is not done if they are regarded as groups with merely limited objectives.[12] A desirable society is the one which allows and sponsors groups and organizations with a life and purpose of their own. There is a hint elsewhere in Lindsay's writings that capitalism in its present form cannot fulfill that function. A socialist society would, therefore, not only preserve individual freedom, but it would make it more concrete by fulfilling human desires "to belong," by providing a variety of groups the purpose and the life of which would be a school for democracy.

There has been in recent political thought a valid criticism of Lindsay's use of pluralism. W. Y. Elliott has pointed out that no "purposive" group can exist only on the basis of its "purpose," and that many of them shift their activity to the achievement of purely economic and social postulates.[13] The danger of a pluralist society whether under socialism or capitalism is, as has been pointed out, the danger of warfare of organized groups for economic and other advantages. A society which admits of excessive intermediate loyalties is always in danger in having both the state and individual freedom suffer at the hands of powerful interests. What remains as a valuable part of Lindsay's formulation is his echoing of Bosanquet's observation that the state has a moral purpose, and it is indeed impossible to conceive any point of departure for social or economic reform unless this be it.

Laski's position is a clear antithesis of any moral significance of the state. A state is for him only "a collection of men and women." To ascribe to this collection any mythical or moral importance is beyond him. There is no General Will. "The will of the State" is the will of certain people who have imposed their power over the society. Like any other institution the state exists to perform certain duties. It is solely to be judged on the basis of its performance.[14]

It is pertinent to ask whether such views can be reconciled with socialism. The latter assumes that at least during the period of transition the state (for instance, in liquidating capitalism) acts as an agent of the common purpose. It is easy to debunk the

---

[12] *Ibid.*, pp. 38–39.
[13] Elliott, *Pragmatic Revolt in Politics*, pp. 369 ff.
[14] *Proceedings of the Aristotelian Society*, Suppl., VIII, 57.

state, but then it is difficult to argue that the interest of the community should take precedence over that of a smaller group. It is curious that Laski's argument along utilitarian lines should land him in a sort of pluralism of interest groups, while Lindsay, who used the arguments of Bosanquet and Green, should also approach pluralism but of a different variety.

Underlying this strongly academic discussion is a very concrete dilemma of the modern state. Increasingly the state is assumed to have some specific duties which go beyond the concept of preserving and enforcing public order. One does not have to be a socialist to see certain constructive duties of the state. It has to eradicate illiteracy and expand the education of its citizens. It is supposed to provide a certain minimum of economic well-being for every citizen. How far, in achieving these objectives, is the state justified in doing violence to the feelings or actual freedom of its citizens whether considered individually or as groups, professional, religious, or economic in their character? To mention a most concrete example, the state is generally assumed to have certain responsibilities in regard to public health. Can it in pursuing this objective impose certain duties and a form of organization upon the medical profession? For Laski, presumably, the question exists only as a question of pragmatic politics. If the majority of the electorate delivers the mandate for a given policy then the problem is solved. But even as a question of pragmatic politics the issue is far from solved. There are issues on which a segment of the population will submit to a bare majority of its countrymen, and there are issues on which an overwhelming majority will not have its way without a profound disturbance. The value of Lindsay's insight lies in his realization of the problem. Men to be sure will resent decisions of the state which hurt, or which they think hurt, their interests. But their attitude will be influenced by the consideration whether the state is acting, however mistakenly, as the representative of the common interest or as an instrument of class interest. In other words, a state can undertake a far-reaching program of social reform and preserve democracy only if the character of its actions is such that it is absolved from the charge that it is acting as an instrument of sectional interests. To state the problem is one thing and to solve it, or even to indicate the ways of solving it, is another. It is a mistake to think that socialism can remain democratic merely by being linked to a simple majority principle. Such a conception is not only fallacious, but it is also impractical under the machinery of a democratic state like Great Britain. Lindsay's view implies that the victory of a new philosophy of government is determined not by a success at the polls or by legislative acts, but by a conscious rethinking of certain moral and social questions by a vast majority of the citizens. He brings out the element which is never absent from socialist thought but which is often deëmphasized by the attention given to other issues: new social forms must be accompanied by a readjustment in human thinking. It is not a futile plea for changing human nature but an appeal for bringing out its social and altruistic elements, often suppressed by political and economic institutions.

Where does constitutionalism fit into the picture? Bosanquet was too ready to translate his theory of the General Will into a legalistic theory of sovereignty. In other words, by arguing for increased functions and powers of the community we do not necessarily argue for an Austinian theory of sovereignty, and certainly we do not have to go to the lengths advocated by Bosanquet when he was ready to justify any and all state actions whatever their moral basis. Lindsay's concept of constitutionalism is a comfortable one: his "constitution" is not properly speaking a legal document, but a statement of purposes and ideals of a society. Here the issue is avoided; a constitution is really much more than that: it is a formal or informal description of a form of government, and of its machinery, and a body of rules often designed to limit powers of the government. To a "practical" socialist like Mr. Laski, constitutional forms are sometimes a nuisance. Constitutions when they work are most often the ways of holding up progress and one of Bosanquet's sins is "making legal claims ethical in substance." [15] Endowing the fabric of any state with special sanctity is distasteful to the utilitarian tradition to which Mr. Laski and his brand of socialism belong.

The whole discussion has a significance beyond its academic pretext. Socialism, its critics often and unfairly remark, has few

[15] *Ibid.*, p. 49.

constructive elements in it; most of its energies are poured into vituperation and attack upon the status quo. While this is patently absurd, socialism does have a real problem in formulating its attitude towards the state. What happens when the state begins moving towards socialism? Is it then the embodiment of the General Will, as Lindsay would hold with some reservations, or is it still an artificial collection of men and women as Laski will have it? If the latter view is adopted, what moral claims can the state have upon its citizens in excess of the few rights "granted" by a socialist to the capitalist state? From the point of view of a socialist the state remains an ambiguous phenomenon. This is true even of the most unregenerate Marxist, for the phrase that the state is an organ of the ruling class does not really answer the question and it confronts a Marxist with a new dilemma when he views a socialist state.

THE MODERN DEMOCRATIC STATE

There comes a point for any political philosophy when it has to go beyond a purely theoretical discussion and into the realm of practical politics. The venture is often undertaken with hesitation, the writer can describe the problems of his own day only, while political philosophy, properly speaking, ought to have a more enduring character. Yet there is a large intermediate area between political philosophy and practical politics. We are somewhat impatient of too many abstractions, and it is only natural that concepts like the General Will, the common good, and so forth, should receive some practical illustration. In turning to Lindsay and to what might be called his school it is useful to examine some of the more concrete proposals and postulates presented by neo-idealism and various strains of non-Marxist socialism which are allied with it.

The word stressed by Lindsay and which reappears with great frequency in the writings of the whole group is "democracy." The implication inherent in the usage is that even the most developed nations of the West, Great Britain and the United States, have not achieved a "real" democracy, and that that happy stage can be brought about not only by political but also by economic and social measures.

Political terminology defies attempts at precision. When we use the word democracy we may mean several things. Politically, the form of government which guarantees to every citizen the right to vote and the possibility of holding a high political office, and which makes this right meaningful, can be described as democracy. We do not have to go to the extravagance of withholding this claim for a country which believes in direct democracy, as Rousseau wanted, or in election to public offices by lot as the Athenians had practiced. Historically, it is a curious fact, there has been until very recent times no school of thought which has set democracy as the main objective of its political theory. The utilitarians, who came closest to doing so, thought of political democracy as an appendage to their main theory and not vice versa. There have been individual thinkers like Rousseau who have formulated democratic postulates, but no group of political writers ever set down and attempted to work out an overall general democratic theory, independent of a specific form of government like Rousseau's. To Marxism or idealism political democracy is not the main element in social structure. Those Marxists and idealists who occupied themselves with the problem thought of democracy as a by-product of a given political or social transformation.

The reason for this hesitation about the most discussed and important term of contemporary politics is rather involved. There is in most political writers an open or concealed elitist bias. At the same time the setting of politics in our age makes a frank, antidemocratic theory impossible. Even the protagonists of Fascism and National Socialism could not make up their mind whether to present their regimes as embodying an antidemocratic principle or as representing the real democracy. A political writer in England or in the United States, if he has doubts about political democracy, about the feasibility of representative government, will keep his doubts to himself. His views will be expressed in his judgments on peripheral subjects: he will attack public opinion or will plead for added responsibilities to be vested in the civil service.

The rationale of representative government is thus seldom defended in itself. Logically any justification for political democracy must be based on an extreme belief in human rationality. Historically political democracy is of a very recent origin. Modern arguments for it, from the Puritan Revolution on, have stressed, not the rational element of human nature, but what might be called the mystic or religious sense in which all men are equal. This argument got engrafted upon politics, and universal suffrage became the pattern of government in the twentieth century. Writers who construed arguments for political democracy were interested in it mainly as a *method of government* which would achieve the desired social or economic objects. The development of party government and the perceptions of writers like Ostrogorski and Michels have served to weaken the belief in political democracy as an effective form of government. Yet the formal structure of political democracy, expressed mainly in universal suffrage, has spread all over the world, and today it is the prevailing pattern of government, both in the countries which have a substantial claim to be considered as political democracies, and in the ones in which it is but a cover for a dictatorial regime. It has been generally recognized by most political writers that the extreme concept of political democracy which assumes not only that every man and woman should have an equal vote, but also that any individual is qualified to discharge any political office, has something of the utopian in it. What is more important, political democracy is assumed today more and more to depend in its effectiveness upon the conditioning factors of social and economic relations.

To return to the group represented by Lindsay and some other writers from the ranks of the Labour Party: they are of the school of thought which is most intensely interested in redefining the concept of political democracy and in discovering the social and economic basis which must underlie it. They reject the conclusions and even more so the tone of Marxism as being detrimental to the development of political democracy. But the doubts and failures sketched above still bother the writers. Lindsay expresses them when he writes

Is Hitler's claim to interpret the spirit of his people more absurd than the claim — repudiated by Bosanquet — that a thing so delicate and complex is interpreted at the polls? Is adult suffrage an integral indispensable part of democratic society, or is it as vestigial as most share-holders' meetings? [16]

The mechanics of a democratic state are assumed to have little significance unless they express a spiritual reality. But what endows political institutions with that reality? The socialist answer to it is that a better society must rest on specific social and economic bases. Private property is to wither away, not completely but as a source of social inequality. Economic stability is secured by the assumption of controls by the state. Socialism is to pervade all spheres of activity, and yet political democracy is to be preserved undiminished.[17] There is here a clear assumption that political democracy is in trouble not because its theory does not suit human nature, but because it is inexpedient to democratize one sphere of human activity — politics — without changing the old patterns in other segments of social activity. Socialism is thus seen as the logical consummation of political democracy. The latter is not disparaged as in much of the Marxist theory, but political democracy is assumed to be incomplete without social democracy — which implies socialism.

In their less euphoric moments the proponents of socialism realize that it is not enough to postulate socialism as a necessary component of "real democracy." Certain basic questions still remain. What is the philosophical foundation of the demand for democracy? How can a great multitude of people really share in the making of decisions on issues on which they are completely uninformed? Here the difficulty would be increased under socialism, as the centralized direction of economic life would require political decisions on a great many specialized and technological problems. How is it feasible to combine a set pattern of economic and social relations with the freedom of political choice which should remain with the electorate? Not all of these questions get answered by Lindsay, but a real effort is made to think through a way out of the dilemmas confronting the theory of democracy.

The philosophical argument for democracy is based on a quasi-religious foundation: men are intrinsically equal as moral beings.

---

[16] Lindsay, *The Modern Democratic State*, p. 250.

[17] This is a paraphrase of a statement in E. F. M. Durbin's *The Politics of Democratic Socialism*, p. 343.

To a cynic the answer might appear as a convenient escape from the dilemma of the earlier liberals who argued for political democracy on pragmatic grounds: the adoption of universal suffrage, they said, would destroy the dominance of interest groups in the state, and would procure more honest and efficient government. But it is clear that the real argument for democracy must rest on a somewhat intangible moral basis. Not that Lindsay discards the traditional arguments, some of them ranging back to Aristotle — for instance, the "shoe-pinching" argument for giving the governed a chance to govern. But the greatest weight is quite properly thrown upon the thesis that it is below human dignity to be ruled without having a voice in one's own destiny, that the function of the citizen is a necessary adjunct of human personality, and that to deprive men of the voice in their own development leads to degeneration of their other faculties. The argument is simply that man is incomplete as a moral being unless he shares in making of political decisions. It is easy to quarrel with the argument or to consider it rather commonplace propaganda, but it is difficult to see on what better ground the argument for political democracy can be propounded.

The urge, which in the past, led political scientists to devise the most minute rules to benefit this or that form of government, is today pretty much discredited. It is recognized that even a **perfect** constitution does not make a perfect state. In looking for the solution of a concrete problem of government we look more for a basis of discussion than for a ready-made device. The problem with which Lindsay wrestles most persistently is the problem of leadership in democracy. The notion of the "common man" being capable of discharging or even of judging the performance of a highly specialized job flies too obviously in the face of reality. The modern state must have technical experts and scientists whose skills are incomprehensible to the multitude. Even the less awe-inspiring jobs of the administrator and the economic expert require experience and a certain freedom from the immediacy of political pressure. "How to connect this knowledge of the few with the spirit of the common life is a puzzling business."[18] The character of certain specialized branches of knowledge, now for good

[18] Lindsay, *The Modern Democratic State,* p. 242.

or bad inextricably involved in government, is such that the gap between the knowledge of the expert and that of the average citizen is unbridgeable and ever growing. One of the greatest obstacles to democracy has been the specialized status of the military, which in nations exposed to frequent wars has separated the army from the control and the state of mind of other citizens. It is not inconceivable that a similar state of isolation could arise in relation to scientific and even economic issues which confront every modern nation. The problem of fitting in specialized knowledge with the decision making by representative institutions is of an enormous complexity. Some liberal and social reformers saw in the specialization of skills required for government a hopeful sign. It would, in their opinion, confine the task of making the most important political decisions to a relatively small and enlightened class. The realm of really crucial political decisions would be preserved from the emotionalism and shifting winds of public favor attending a popular discussion. Such an attitude was not absent in John Stuart Mill. Many twentieth-century liberals and even socialists would agree with the view of J. A. Hobson, who envisaged a democracy equipped with an expert class which drafts laws from its technical knowledge and even decides whether a given proposal should be embodied in law or not.[19] This function is often arrogated to the "impartial" civil service. Many socialists, as we shall see, are not above shifting the focus of political decisions, subtly and unobtrusively, from the people to the expert. What the proponents of such measures don't realize is the fact that the logical fulfillment of the tendency is to be found in an organized political priesthood like that of the Communist Party of the USSR. The first prerequisite for intelligent discussion on the subject is the realization that political decisions will always be made for political reasons. The view that the economic and scientific issues which bear upon politics can be left to the expert is therefore a way of begging the question, for aside from the analysis of the given problem the decision itself must be a political one, which the expert himself is no more qualified to render than the next man. What the arguments for the increased power to the expert or the impartial civil service often conceal is general exasperation with

[19] Hobson, *The Crisis of Liberalism*, p. 85.

political democracy and the desire to keep decision making as far away from representative organs, newspapers, and so forth, as possible.

Lindsay shares in what might be called the elitist bias. But his concern with the spiritual side of the problem of democracy keeps him from going over to the school of thought, or rather the way of thinking, described above. Political leadership is, according to him, a necessary implement of democracy. It may require even a special class which devotes itself to politics. From this point of view the collapse of the old English ruling class is not an unmixed blessing, he implies. But the problem of an elite does not appear as the problem of a specific class used to ruling and the making of decisions. It is rather the need for a body of people who have the time and the inclination to devote themselves to politics, and who have at the same time an *esprit de corps* and tradition which distinguish them from professional politicians. But underlying any form of institutionalized or informal political leadershp must be what Lindsay calls the process of discussion. The word "discussion" is used, one feels, to describe the state of continuous participation in politics by the mass of people. Political decisions no longer touch merely the periphery of our lives. They affect very often the very essence of them. Yet the type of "discussion" which Lindsay demands is not very widespread in democratic societies. The issues of politics are debated at the polls, but in everyday lives the mass of people pay little attention to them. The reason for it is sought in the faulty social structure on which political democracy is engrafted. The contention of any radical or socialist must be that the relatively low level of political interest exhibited by the people is due primarily to their instinctive feeling that the crucial decisions are made by the "others." Once given the stake the people will respond to the challenge. This view may have a great deal to it but it would still leave open the question of raising the level of political life and of resisting the pressure of interest groups (if they should be resisted.) The quality pervading the thinking of Lindsay, and of many other theoreticians of the Labour Party on the subject, is a religious semi-mystic one: the citizens of a modern democracy need to be inoculated by what they call the common life. "It is by living together that men learn what they want and conceive purposes to which they will devote themselves by playing complementary roles in a society in which they are all members." [20] There is a curious but not meaningless tautology in this phrase. The plea for making political democracy a working concept is the same one on which the argument for democracy had been raised: the intrinsic equality of men, and the belief in their moral nature. A society in which the bulk of men would feel that the only inequalities spring from justifiable functional distinctions would be the one in which democracy would "really" work, and where one would see active participation by each citizen in public affairs. Lindsay, like Aristotle, sees man as a political animal, but with this distinction: man's craving for a sense of equality has to be satisfied first, before he is fully willing and qualified to participate in political affairs.

In elucidating his "common-life idea" Lindsay asks for socialism, for "there are in industrial communities inequalities too great for fellowship." [21] But then he reverts also to pluralism. The "discussion" if it is to be meaningful must be preceded and supplemented by the citizen getting his political education in a smaller group with which he is intimately associated. A small trade-union branch or a professional organization provides the best opportunity for opinions to crystallize without the interposition of a demagogue or a continuous pressure of great social forces and organs of opinion. This is not guild socialism or pluralism, strictly speaking, but simply an appreciation of the role of a small group in fashioning individual opinions.

The outline of his views on the democratic process shows the extreme eclecticism of Lindsay's views: he is for state interference in social and economic matters to a point reaching socialism. He is solicitous about individualism and careful to save various intermediate groups and their powers as a help both to the state and to the citizen.

In his thinking Lindsay is a descendant of Green, though he is deeply indebted to Bosanquet, and especially to the latter's rephrasing of Rousseau. The typical weaknesses of the idealist school reappear in Lindsay. Those weaknesses rest in the first

---

[20] Lindsay, *The Modern Democratic State*, p. 240.
[21] *Ibid.*, p. 259.

place on a certain oversimplified concept of politics: man is assumed to be an intellectual if not excessively rational creature; the primary social instinct of man is his desire for sympathy and association; the society which enables men to satisfy those drives cannot fail to achieve a modest utopia. In common with the idealists Lindsay does not go into the international ramifications of politics. It does not occur to him that he reproduces unconsciously the frame of mind which is a legacy from the days of England's undoubted supremacy in the world, and that the virtues of the social changes he recommends might be detrimental in a competitive and disturbed world. Essentially, the philosophy of neo-idealism does not escape the nostalgic note of a certain resentment against the industrial society where bigness and purely technical accomplishments can become the conditions for survival. It is an oversimplified but still useful conclusion about most of modern British political thought, whether conservative or radical, that it does not profess to understand or like the industrial age. The phenomenon may be a sort of psychological compensation for Britain's decline from her industrial supremacy, but it is essentially a continuation of the characteristics inherent in British political thought even when Great Britain was at the apex of her commercial and industrial power, and which can be seen not only in Coleridge or Carlyle, but also in John Stuart Mill and in the earliest works of Herbert Spencer. On the other hand Lindsay shows a greater awareness of social problems than did Bosanquet or Green. His theory cannot be accused of disregarding social questions. What can be said against Lindsay's thesis is that he does not appreciate the importance of purely organic factors in politics. He has too much of the philosopher and too little of the historian in him. Great social questions like the adoption of socialism and the development of a democratic "elite" are treated by him merely as problems affected only by human will and reason, and unconnected with the material resources at the disposal of a given society.

The element of great value in the type of thinking exhibited above lies in its preoccupation with a redefinition of democracy. The basic insight of Rousseau, which has served both democrats and antidemocrats, was simply that man seeks in the state an outlet for his desire to associate and coöperate, and that this fact is a stronger element of social cohesion than fear or property. The idealist school built upon that insight a superstructure showing how the instinct which makes society possible can be developed to make it perfect. Lindsay rejects the ready identification of the General Will with sovereignty, and by doing some violence to Rousseau's original concept, prefers to see the manifestation of the General Will in certain acts of popular opinion and feeling. Developing this idea a bit farther we might see the General Will in such prosaic facts as the reorientation of modern democratic opinion towards the idea of the welfare state and the consequent approach to collectivism. The non-Marxist socialist sees the General Will as tending towards socialism, and in Lindsay socialism becomes not a necessary consequence of material developments, but a moral necessity. The achievement of socialism is divorced from the growth of the forces of production and becomes linked to the growing conviction in the minds of men that a form of socialism is a prerequisite to a better society. While on the surface this seems like a rephrasing of some utopian socialism, it acquires a different meaning when injected into a political movement which has achieved power through democratic means.

6

The Theory of Reform

INTRODUCTION

A social scientist or a political philosopher is somewhat like a doctor without any coercive powers over his patient. He often prescribes a medicine or a treatment in full knowledge that the patient will not follow his advice. The voice of a reformer is sometimes listened to for reasons which are often quite unconnected with the ones which underlie his argument for reform. For one thing popularity of a theory may be achieved as a by-product of a war or another kind of social upheaval, and under circumstances which the theory completely failed to envisage or to which it cannot easily be adjusted.

The principles of idealism, of Fabian and guild socialism fell for most part upon the arid soil of academic discussion. In studying the development of British politics over the first third of the twentieth century one must be struck by the reflection how impotent, *in normal times,* are political theories as against set patterns of political life. There is indeed the optical illusion of a correspondence of idealism to the enhanced role of the state, between the increasing interest in socialism and the development and growth of the Labour Party. But the rise of the welfare state has been mainly occasioned by the very practical circumstances of Britain's changed economic situation, the First World War, and the postwar depressions. The Labour Party arose as the product of practical grievances of the trade unions; it absorbed or dwarfed into still further insignificance various tiny groups of doctrinaire socialists in Great Britain, and until 1918 it persisted, as a body, in distrusting even the rudimentary tenets of socialism. If there is a connection between various phenomena in the body politic and political theory, it is likely that the latter is symptomatic of the same social forces which sooner or later bring about political changes. But there is no causal connection, at first, between political changes and political theory. Had Great Britain continued, in the twentieth century, its nineteenth-century pace of economic expansion, had there been no war, then the theories of Green and Bosanquet would have the antiquarian interest of those of Southey and Ruskin, and the *Fabian Essays* would be ranged side by side with the projects of Robert Owen. But then had the seeds of future developments not been inherent in the late nineteenth century probably we would not have had the theories of Green, Bosanquet, or the *Fabian Essays.*

It is when the march of events and the tendency of a political theory coalesce that the latter acquires significance as a reinforcer and a directive. And when the walls of political and social customs crumble it is then that political theories acquire an importance of their own, and compete to become the main ingredient of the new social structure.

The type of political theory offered by idealism consisted mainly in political philosophy which sought the fundamental basis of the state with some strictures about the economic and social sides of political life. The *Fabian Essays,* in contrast, assumed what might be called the historical approach towards the problems of the state. Yet their emphasis upon economic determinism, much milder than that of Marxism, concealed an essentially moralistic approach to politics. The bulk of guild socialism, which is a product of the twentieth century, discards both the economic determinism and the search for understanding of the modern state. Guild socialism is largely the philosophy of social protest without any economic or historical spine, and it is no wonder that it could not hold the allegiance even of its founders, and that some of its utterances[1] create today the impression of incredible naïveté.

It will be seen that none of the social philosophies mentioned above possesses the primary characteristics of a philosophy of reform: a preoccupation with very concrete problems of contemporary politics, and a chart for immediate application of its principles. With the exception of the guild socialists none of the schools of thought mentioned above fancied itself as a vanguard of a political movement. The theories all share in the complacent assumption that the only task of politics is a redirection of the state towards a given pattern of social justice. The machinery of the state, the problem of foreign relations, and the question of the economic efficiency of a given society are by and large left out of the picture. The optimism of the nineteenth century still leaves its residue in modern British political thought. The philosophy which most skillfully blends various trends of thought, that of Lindsay's neo-idealism, exhibits the same cheerful disregard of the organic factors of politics. To a certain extent this is understandable; it is not the task of a political philosopher to formulate party platforms or to worry about budgets. At the same time there is a condition of realism which political theory should strive to observe in its assumptions. It is not surprising therefore that much of the political philosophy of today emanates from the writings of economists and of people concerned with the practical issues of political administration. At the time of crisis, when political theory could be of immediate importance, its influence has appeared to be in creating the assumptions and prejudices which lie in the back of the minds of economists and administrators when they devise the "practical" solutions.

In fact the influence of political theory upon political practice is likely to be somewhat intangible, especially in Great Britain where a major party cannot afford to remain doctrinaire, since it has to take its turn in governing the country. Political power creates its own atmosphere and its own interests. The effect of theories, along with that of the social background of the leaders, lies mainly in creating the frame of analysis of the given problems,

---

[1] E.g., Bertrand Russell's *Proposed Roads to Freedom* (New York, 1919).

rather than in creating new problems. The problems and policies of the Labour government of today are not explained by the theories of Green or the Fabians, but the way the government leaders analyze and approach their problems, and the philosophical foundation of the economics they follow, are not without a direct relationship to the type of thinking which idealism and socialism have encouraged.

The tenor of British politics has always been unfriendly to purely doctrinaire parties. As mentioned above the "invention" of parliamentary government has had the effect of purging the major parties of doctrinaire radicalism or conservatism, as they have had to take their turn in ruling the country and the empire and in confronting practical problems not susceptible of doctrinaire solution. It is interesting to note how this fact has distorted British public thinking on foreign affairs. It was assumed in 1933 that the acquisition of power would have a "sobering" effect upon Hitler. The same assumption can be seen in the emancipation of parts of the Empire, in the turning over of political power to the most extreme nationalist elements, as in India where the assumption has proved correct until now (summer 1950) and in Burma where it has had disastrous results.

The usual explanation for this even temper of British politics has been commonly found in the thesis about the "agreement on fundamentals," which held that the major parties agreed on the fundamentals of political democracy and private property, and consequently have been able to displace each other in power without the danger of friction or civil strife. The academic question which the writers of textbooks on British government loved to pose was what would happen if a party arose and succeeded to power with a set of assumptions running against the notions of the agreement on fundamentals?

It can be seen that the idea underlying the thesis is something of an oversimplification. There have been during the past century and a half some pretty fundamental disagreements between major political movements in Great Britain. The "fundamentals" of 1832 were not the same as those of the 1880's. No responsible statesman in the nineteenth century would have believed that a time would come when the maximum income-tax rate would reach 92½ per cent, and if he could have envisaged that he would have added that the country would then be torn by a civil war. Essentially, the notion of the agreement on fundamentals misses the dynamic character of political development in a democracy. Democracy has harnessed the process of revolution to that of orderly government. The threat to the continuity of that process comes not from political doctrines, no matter how extreme, but from the pressure of objective circumstances, like economic depression at home, or military threats from abroad.

The rise and fortunes of the Labour Party demonstrate the moderating influence of the democratic process (a Communist would say the corrupting influence). The party arose from the needs and desires of the trade unions. The cause of the separate political movement of the working classes can be sought in many facts such as the extension of franchise, the weakening of British economy, specific legal grievances like the Taff Vale decision, and so forth. But one may hazard a theory that it was not so much a sense of legal oppression or enmity toward the two established parties (which were always ready to bargain with and seek friends with the Labour movement) which persuaded the trade unions to break up with their previous traditions, as it was the feeling of the strangeness and separateness from the working class of the social milieu from which the Conservatives and the Liberals drew their leadership. The birth of the Labour Party signified the social emancipation of the British working class, and was the direct result of the system which beneath very real political democracy had preserved not only the trappings but also the spirit of social inequality.

It is therefore not surprising that the most elemental and noticeable characteristic of the Labour Party has been the drive towards the vague but exciting notion of social equality. The leadership of the party for a long time had been largely drawn from the earlier constituted and much more radical socialist group, the Independent Labour Party.

Yet the character of the Labour Party has not been unaffected by these considerations. After the First World War it soon achieved the status of the official opposition, with brief periods in office, but without an absolute majority in the House of Com-

mons. It developed an official philosophy — not without the opposition of its trade union elements — of a socialist variety with a
Fabian flavor.

The relationship of the Labour Party to the practices and conventions of British parliamentary life was the subject of much
discussion prior to 1945. We shall see later on the reaction of some
of the most responsible leaders to the events of 1931, when they
felt the party was tricked out of office and its most prominent
members were captured by the Tories. But the most important
question has always been the problem of reconciling the existence
of a political party which advocates a definite change in the social
and economic system with the very existence of party government
and the two-party system. On the surface the problem looks in-
soluble: if the Labour Party should during its term of office initiate
reforms running counter to the basic philosophy of the party
which then succeeds it in power, what happens then? Is the
reform undone with complete chaos to follow, or is the Conservative Party to abdicate its role and to carry on the socialist state
until the Labour Party again takes over and initiates a new wave of
reforms? But the process of politics has a logic of its own, and the
fear of violent alternations in the type of government, depending
upon which party is in power, has been proved groundless in
Great Britain, at least until today. The problem has been put in a
somewhat absurd fashion by some of the Labour Party's theoreticians.[2] Any political measure which shows its usefulness or which
becomes a part of the pattern of social development is not likely
to be discarded by a mere shift in political power. Whether this
fact is in itself desirable or not, whether it shows the politicians'
desire to accommodate themselves to popular prejudices rather
than to stick by their principles is another matter. But there is no
doubt that this has been the pattern of political development in
Great Britain and the United States, and that it has made possible
the preservation of democratic government.[3]

[2] See Barker's condemnation of Laski's view that "the continuance of parliamentary government would depend upon its [Labour's] possession of guarantees
that its work of transformation would not be disrupted by repeal in the event of its
defeat at the polls." *Reflections on Government*, p. 183.
[3] For a discussion of the problem see Durbin, *Politics of Democratic Socialism*,
pp. 306–313.

The task of government is conceived today in dynamic terms. This commonplace has some significance, for even the liberal theory of the nineteenth century envisaged the process of governing as a static one, once the abuses had been curbed and the needed reforms had been installed. But today no political party would admit that its platform should contain no startling innovations to be adopted into law once the party is in power. This situation has a peculiar significance to a socialist and democratic party. By virtue of its philosophy it has to advance very fast in order to preserve its distinctive mark. Unlike a conservative or a liberal party it cannot measure its achievements merely by the quality of its administration, or even by the condition of the country under its rule. There is always another fraction of the ideal to be realized. Socialist ministers are much more the slaves of their program than are their conservative counterparts.

More important than the ideology is the set of prejudices and preconceptions which act upon people's minds. No matter how Machiavellian a politician might wish to be he cannot, in ordinary circumstances, shake off completely the effect of the doctrines he has professed and advocated. In studying the policies of a government one has to keep in mind that both the men who make them and the men who have to approve of them are not a group of logicians confronting a set of objective facts, but that the facts and the policies appear to them through the necessarily distorted prism of their social background and the theories they got used to when not in power. It is fitting therefore to examine some examples of the theories which lie directly in the background of the Labour Party.

THE SOCIALIST COMMONWEALTH

The purely mechanical aspect of government does not attract the reformer of today as much as it used to in the nineteenth century. We have grown weary of constitution making, and of the notion that the welfare of a nation depends upon a cleverly constructed clause. The search for the best means of reform is likely to embrace schemes of economic change rather than various devices for changing the legislature, and so forth. Furthermore, in the purely political field there are as of today (and the same was true except for full women's suffrage in the 1920's) very few institutions or issues which call for further democratization or change. A few alterations in the franchise (of which the Labour government of 1945 has taken care), the perplexing but no longer primarily important question of the House of Lords — these are all that remain in the way of structural problems for British democracy. The institution of monarchy has never been questioned by responsible socialist leaders, and it has shown remarkable powers of accommodation to the changing world, which together with its emotional and traditional appeal, would make any attack upon it useless and mischievous.

Nevertheless, prior to its assumption of power the Labour Party often tackled the problem of a constitutional change. In this respect as in many others, the theoreticians of the Labour movement are ideological descendants of Jeremy Bentham and his school.

Bentham himself has been classified as a prototype of bourgeois liberalism and in a sense this is true. His liberalism, however, was not a conscious defence of business interests. He faced a typical dilemma of the social reformer: how to reconcile what might be called a long-run view of social justice with the needs of an immediate improvement of society. The logic of his calculus seemed to imply that an equal distribution of wealth would be the surest way to "maximize" happiness. Yet would not the happiness of the society, the whole prospect of reform, be endangered if the security of well-to-do citizens were threatened? Logic and the practical instinct, the bias of a bourgeois and the faith of a philosopher seemed inextricably bound together in contradictions and conflicts. Here the spirit of the century saved him from an embarrassing dilemma. For it was an era which believed in progress and Bentham could proclaim that time is a great mediator. In a prosperous nation there was to be a constant progress towards equality, provided that laws would not counteract this tendency by shackling industry, creating monopolies, and so forth.[4] Freed of his social and economic dilemma Bentham could go on proposing various political reforms, the spirit if not the mechanics of which were to leave their imprint upon British history.

[4] Bentham, *Theory of Legislation,* ed. G. R. Ogden (London 1931), pp. 104 ff.

More than a hundred years afterwards a new constitution was proposed by two people whose researches into the social history of England had convinced them that Bentham's original assumption was faulty and that socialism was the only solution for the evils of the now mature capitalist economy and political structure. The attempt of Sidney and Beatrice Webb to draw a blueprint has today only historical interest though it was formulated right after the First World War. With the assumption of its responsibilities as a major party Labour has turned towards more pressing problems. But the effort remains an interesting commentary on the theoretical approach of two people who in their historical investigations showed a great deal of realism, and one of whom was soon to hold important offices of the state.

The work is pervaded by much of the reforming zeal and idealism characteristic of a party which has not as yet shouldered the responsibilities of government. We are told solemnly that the Socialist Commonwealth will replace the "stuffiness of private interests" with the new reign of "Measurement and Publicity." [5] The central thesis of the book is, however, the one which remains the motto of the Labour Party:

But the central wrong of the capitalist system is neither the poverty of the poor, nor the riches of the rich; it is the power which the mere ownership of the instruments of production gives to a relatively small section of the community over the actions of their fellow citizens and over the mental and physical environment of successive generations.[6]

Socialism is, perhaps, easily recommendable on purely moral grounds. The question most often raised in relation to its successful adoption is the question of the practicability of achieving postulates which may be very desirable on purely ethical grounds. From the perspective of the achievement of the Labour government in the first five years of its rule (and under circumstances which make an appraisal of this achievement exceedingly difficult), the mere fact of undermining the old attitudes and incentives of a society may have a depressing effect on its economy. The problem of transi-

[5] S. and B. Webb, A Constitution for the Socialist Commonwealth, London, 1920, p. 356.
[6] Ibid., introduction, p. xii.

tion from capitalism to socialism has been neglected by most socialist writers. The practical difficulties of changing men's motivations
loom almost insurmountable. It can be truly said that every social
system creates its own problems, and that no amount of writing
and theorizing can foresee the type of situation which will arise
under changing social conditions.

The error into which the Webbs fall, and it is a characteristic
mistake of many reformers, is the assumption that any reform di-
rected towards the goal of social justice and equality is of necessity accompanied by desirable changes in human motivations. It
is amazing to see how excessively a reformer often conceives human
beings to be the slaves of their institutions, and yet how readily
he concedes that once the institutions change there would be no
lag in a complete reorientation of men's incentives and attitudes.
Men are conceived of as entirely rational and endowed with a
passion for equality. Free them from the domination of interests
and the degradation of a social system which bars inequality,
and you will have a great outpouring of constructive social endeavor.

The means to be used in the process of reconstruction do not
meet the strict constitutional test: "Especially during the stage of
transition from a predominantly capitalist society it may be necessary to prohibit the publication of newspapers with the object of
private profit or under individual ownership as positively dangerous to the community." [7] This statement, hardly qualified by
the concession that some unofficial press (run like consumers'
coöperatives) may be allowed to stay, is rather ill becoming to
writers who assert that decisions in a socialist society would be
reached on a democratic basis and that "this common consent will
be reached by the cogency of accurately ascertained and authoritatively reported facts driven home by the silent persuasiveness
of the public opinion of those concerned." [8]

A little slip of the nature quoted above is characteristic. It
shows a certain intellectual arrogance combined with political
naïveté. It is not only that the socialists are not to be heckled while
they proceed solemnly with the task of bringing social justice and

[7] *Ibid.*, p. 270.
[8] *Ibid.*, p. 196.

efficiency, but also that they are assumed to be free from the normal human frailties consequent upon holding power. There is a tinge of bureaucratic stuffiness not without an element of unconscious humor in the phrase about "authoritatively reported facts." But perhaps socialism of any variety, like any semireligious social creed, demands a certain solemnity which deprives its devotees of a sense of humor.

The work is pervaded by the notion of categories and classifications. The democratic organization of the community must rest not on the human being as such, but rather on a fourfold division of man: man as producer; man as consumer; man as citizen, here subdivided into (a) the citizen concerned with defence against aggression, internal or external, and (b) the citizen concerned with the promotion of the type of civilization he desires, and with the material and nonmaterial interests of future generations.[9]

The classification does not require much comment. It shows clearly the basic rationalistic prejudice of the authors. It is doubtful whether the complexity of man's interests can be so neatly separated and institutionalized. It is doubtful, for instance, whether something so intangible as man's stake in the "nonmaterial interests of the future generations" can be set against something so concrete as his interests as a consumer.

The division leads to the proposal to distribute the field of legislation between two parliaments: one "political," the other one "social." To the political body are left the powers over foreign relations, defence, and police. It has its own committee — the Cabinet. The Premier's power to dissolve this parliament is subject to certain limitations.[10]

The social parliament is a much more important body. It regulates economic life (including taxation), and education. It has no clearly separated executive, but it is to be run like an English municipal council with committees supervising relevant administrative branches "without the various chairmen necessarily agreeing with each other in policy, or accepting as such any responsibility for the work of other committees than their own." [11]

---

[9] *Ibid.*, introduction, p. xvii.
[10] *Ibid.*, p. 117.
[11] *Ibid.*, p. 120.

It is not subject to dissolution except at a request of a majority of its members.

That the two bodies may conflict is something of an afterthought of the scheme, which seems to combine the most unworkable features of several parliamentary systems. The social parliament is to organize public services, the political one to prescribe their use and devise regulations. The political body has to have its expenditures approved by the social parliament. Should a "jurisdictional" conflict occur, the courts would arbitrate.[12]

That the book was written in 1920 may be taken as a partial justification of the unrealism pervading its recommendations. It is unconceivable that a person, no matter what his political persuasion, who has had experience in running a ministry should abandon the singleness of direction and the consequent unity of policy characteristic of the British system. The cumbersome machinery devised to run the state, the abandonment of ministerial responsibility, the division of power between two bodies which, though elected on a similar basis, are almost certain to run into continuous conflicts — all these details, though inspired by most worthwhile motives, show a mechanistic and unreal concept of government.

What is behind this confusion? One reason for it may be an attempt to appease the guild socialists (although the social parliament, unlike Cole's Commune, is not elected by functional organizations). But the basic reason is a strange belief that politics and party government are not necessary elements of democracy. The process of governing is to be exorcised of politics. The groups of planners and civil servants are to make their decisions on "factual" and scientific bases. Nothing is more naïve than this attempt and the accompanying assumption that economics can be separated from politics. The imagined gain to liberty would in all probability prove illusory since the social parliament holding the purse strings would become a more powerful body than its political counterpart.

In the general pattern of economic life, the Webbs go back to the gradualness and moderation of the *Fabian Essays*. Socialism is not to embrace the whole field of economy. Agriculture (that is, small holdings), smaller industrial enterprises, and even some

[12] *Ibid.*, p. 123.

major industries (those "for the sake of comparative costs") are to be exempted from public ownership.[13] The pattern of nationalization, again, reminds one of the *Fabian Essays*. There is to be a national board running each nationalized industry and appointed by the social parliament. The Webbs reject the claims of guild socialism.[14] There must be autonomy for every "vocation" and it is to be represented on the national board of the relevant industry, but it is the expert who is to give guidance to industrial life. The proposals bear a close affinity to the measures actually adopted by the Labour Government after 1945. In the field of economic policy the book still has relevance to the present situation, though its purely constitutional and structural recommendations have been happily forgotten.

For all its limitations this concept of a socialist commonwealth is remarkably free of purely doctrinaire ideas, while at the same time it reflects a certain bureaucratic mentality in its authors. It is rather touching to see a socialist disputing the contention that man is inspired exclusively by the craving for riches and giving the learned professions and the British Civil Service as examples to the contrary. The spirit of parliamentary institutions eludes the Webbs. The House of Commons is the seat of administrative institutions for them.[15] To those brought up in a strictly administrative tradition parliamentary bodies are talking shops. They are likewise unable to see the need for political parties once the country reaches the higher stage of democracy embodied in socialism. The result is a society run by committees and civil servants. In contrast with Marxian socialism the pattern of this type of socialism is all reasonability and moderation, but the generating power of enthusiasm and the religious zeal of a great social transformation are irretrievably lost. The pattern proposed in the Webbs' book envisages an undynamic society, where social security and as much of economic equality as possible are the key mottoes. The emphasis on administration is not unimportant. A great deal of the actual program of the Labour Party has been formulated by

[13] *Ibid.*, p. 148.
[14] "The plain truth is that Democracies of Producers cannot be trusted with the ownership of production in their own vocation. Each vocation, however important it may be, is but a fragment of the community." *Ibid.*, p. 156.
[15] *Ibid.*, p. 355.

people who (especially many of the Fabians) either had themselves been civil servants or admired the achievements of the civil service in the country which formulated its modern concept.

Insofar as the later development of the Labour Party is concerned the Webbs' book has had little influence. The party has never seriously undertaken to tamper with the traditional constitutional machinery, except to weaken still farther the House of Lords. The virtue of an "omnicompetent" House of Commons lies among other things in the ease with which a far-reaching program of reform can be carried out even with the slimmest popular mandate. It is not therefore surprising that the most insistent pleas for weakening what amounts to a virtual monopoly of the House of Commons in legislation have come from the Conservatives. The outline for a socialist constitution has remained on paper, but it is still a valuable piece of evidence of the state of mind of British socialism in the twenties, and the intellectual atmosphere in which the Webbs concocted their fantastic ideas has not as yet completely vanished.

THE PLANNED ECONOMY AND FREE SOCIETY

The growth of the doctrine that freedom is a positive concept rather than a negative one and that it consists of opportunities for self-expression rather than of the lack of constraints upon liberty, has corresponded to the growth of a new system of political economy. A layman may be indeed excused for suspecting the economists, who, like other human beings, formulate their judgments in social matters upon political assumptions generated by the spirit of the period. The fact remains that for all practical purposes the way of thinking about economics which has been variously called laissez faire or economic liberalism is dead and buried. The economic system which sprang up during the dominance of economic liberalism is still very much alive, and socialism has still to prove that it can replace capitalism in a way which would provide a more efficient economy, or, on the political and social side, a more humane and democratic society. But the defenders of capitalism except for a few die-hards no longer use the arguments which would have pleased Jeremy Bentham or David Ricardo. The notion that the very momentum of material progress will of

itself without regulation or direction secure ever increasing prosperity and equitable distribution of goods has been discredited. It
is useless, from our point of view, to inquire whether the systems
of laissez faire ever had a fair trial or whether theoretically it still
remains a valid economic theory. The important thing for a
political scientist is to see what considerations regulate the political thinking and behavior of people rather than to point out the
economic soundness or unsoundness of such considerations. It is
easy in contemplating the vicissitudes of various theories to put
the main burden of social change upon the power and persuasiveness of a few writers. Lord Keynes, one of the makers of the revolution in economic thinking, took an extreme point of view on that
question.[16] But it is doubtful, had Keynes preached his ideas in the
middle of the nineteenth century, that he would have been regarded as anything but a harmless eccentric. The independent
power of ideas, whether political or economic, is an optical illusion. They are powerful insofar as they crystallize and formulate
the notions which the course of social developments has led the
people to grope for.

In the case of Keynes and his school the political assumption
which underlay the economic reorientation was simply the enhanced power and function of the state. In the face of the recurrent economic crises which troubled the world after the First
World War it was inconceivable that the old notion that the
state can do nothing positive to influence the course of national
economy should survive. The new economic philosophy had also
a pleasing social undertone: the functional defect of a highly in-
dustrialized society was diagnosed as a maldistribution of income,
and the consequent propensity to oversave. The old views of J. A.
Hobson, held by a majority of economists to be eccentric when
they were first formulated, now found their way into an economic

[16] "The ideas of economists and political philosophers, both when they are right
and when they are wrong, are more powerful than is commonly understood. Indeed
the world is ruled by little else. Practical men who believe themselves to be quite
exempt from any intellectual influences, are usually the slaves of some defunct
economists. Madmen in authority, who hear voices in the air, are distilling their
frenzy from some academic scribbler of a few years back. I am sure that the power
of vested interests is vastly exaggerated compared with the gradual encroachment
of ideas. Not indeed immediately . . . But soon or late it is ideas not vested interests, which are dangerous for good or evil." J. M. Keynes, *The General Theory
of Employment, Interest, and Money,* p. 383.

theory which was soon to influence not only professors, but also government circles in Great Britain and the United States. The new way of thinking about economics has presented an aspect of political and social eclecticism which has brought into its fold many of the defenders of capitalism as well as believers in complete state domination of economic life.[17]

At first it might appear, as many Marxist economists hold, that the general tendency of Keynesian economics is to set up a halfway system designed to save capitalism and consequently that most socialists would see it as a direct rival to their own creed. The fact remains that the economic postulates of the theory bear a close resemblance to the preliminary goals of evolutionary socialism. The Keynesian system is susceptible of advance towards the welfare state. It places upon the government the main responsibility for the level of consumption, it encourages a drastic redistribution of income by means of taxation, and it does not in itself contain anything antithetical towards the ultimate goals of socialism. Believers in economic individualism have execrated the system as destroying, in a more subtle and dangerous way than a frontal attack could do, the very basis upon which capitalism is founded, but it is difficult to see in the new economics anything else but the description and logical implementation of the road the modern state has followed in the past fifty years.

Looking closer at the political implications of the economic system recommended by Keynes and his school, one must recognize that it accentuates the tendency of which it is the product. The stress upon the possibilities of state manipulation of economic life strengthens the tendency towards economic nationalism. International trade, which original liberalism conceived as a great agency of human progress and of peace, becomes again an arena of rivalry. The principle that the state should provide a modicum of livelihood for every citizen has certainly great humanitarian as

[17] "Thus I agree with Gesell that the result of filling in the gaps in the classical theory is not to dispose of the 'Manchester System' but to indicate the nature of the environment which the free play of economic forces requires if it is to realize the full potentialities of production. The central controls necessary to ensure full employment will, of course, involve a large extension of the traditional functions of government . . . But there will still remain a wide field for the exercise of private initiative and responsibility. Within this field the traditional advantages of individualism will still hold good." *Ibid.*, p. 379.

well as political value. But the price paid for the acceptance of the principle is not only an increased interference by the state in everyday life, but also the evaluation of political power even in short-run terms on the basis of one criterion — the success of the government in raising the standard of living. To be sure political actions have always been evaluated, largely, in terms of their economic effects. But by placing a definite responsibility upon the state, and by implying to the popular mind that economic progress is only a result of clever manipulation by the state, the new theory of economics goes far in subjecting political motivation to the considerations of economic security and comfort. Such a result would have been deemed undesirable to the school which pioneered the notion of state interference in economic matters — the idealists who thought of economic well-being as means to an end, but certainly not as an all-absorbing aim. Popular concepts of the type mentioned above diverge also from the ideal of socialism, which preaches the abolition of capitalism not only because it is an inefficient way of producing and distributing goods to the whole community, but because it involves an unjust and immoral system of private property and social differentiation. It is therefore an open question how far the type of thinking engendered by Keynes' theories, congenial as it is to the atmosphere in which socialism and especially democratic socialism grows, is compatible with the ultimate aspirations to which socialism adheres and the type of strategy these aspirations may require. A social philosophy has always certain ultimate ends which transcend purely material objectives. Insofar as a philosophy of this kind allies itself with a policy designed to produce immediate and concrete results, it may eventually become subjugated to the latter and sacrifice its ultimate perspective for a series of short-run practical successes which bring the state and society no nearer to the original goal of the philosophy. This consideration explains the doctrinaire voices which are heard from time to time addressing the Labour Government and urging it to forget the economic strictures of Keynes and the present state of the country's economy, and to attain the objective of socialism, no matter what the immediate price may be. A strongly ideological party attaining power is always in a difficult situation. It has to oscillate between the poetry of its pro-

gram and the prosaic demands of administration and politics with
angry voices on both sides proclaiming betrayal of national welfare to doctrinaire considerations and of principles to expediency.
Under democratic principles, there is, furthermore, no possibility
of conducting the experiment under controlled conditions. The
party has to satisfy the small core of its followers, who are socialists because of faith, but also the much vaster group of followers
who base their allegiance on the performance of the government.

We have tried to point out here the socio-political implications
of economic theories expounded by Keynes and his school. As in
the case of the liberal economics propounded by Adam Smith,
Ricardo, and the following generation of British economists it is
not the strict theory which is important in this connection but the
way in which both governmental measures and popular thinking
are influenced by the atmosphere and political assumptions of such
thinking.

Nearer to a purely economic question is the problem of how
far Keynes' theories are applicable to the type of economy Great
Britain emerged with in 1945. Isn't the new theory unsuitable to a
country which has to reëquip its industry and practically to ac-
cumulate new capital, in a world where the normal springs of
international investment are dried up? How far is the preoccupation with economic security favorable to the development of those
parts of the commonwealth which have a low economic potential
due to their small population or capital? It is perhaps easy to see
that had our present economic mentality triumphed in the middle
of the nineteenth century with all its paraphernalia of elaborate
trade unionism and government regulations, the economic development of Great Britain and the United States would have been
more in accordance with humanitarian ideas, but would have proceeded, by the same token, at a much slower pace. Economic
theories do not any more than their political counterparts exist in
a vacuum. They find their moorings in the factors of psychology of
the given people. The slow growth to supremacy of the principle
of state interference as against the principle of economic individualism represents a deliberate choice of political democracy,
or, as a political philosopher would be tempted to put it, of the
General Will. But it is clear that as the shift from mercantilist to

"free trade" economy brought with it a variety of economic and political changes unthought of by the economists when they propounded their new theories, so the new change of economic mentality is bringing with it vast political changes which as yet may not be seen in their full import.

Keynes' book, appearing in 1936, collected the hints of his previous works in a systematic exposition of the mechanical faults of capitalism. It is beside the question, here, to ask whether Keynes' critique is valid or whether it does not generalize a psychological weakness of capitalism as it appeared between the two world wars into a general condemnation of its ability to keep up a high level of employment. Keynes' *General Theory* served to crystallize the type of searching criticism of capitalism which had existed since the Great Depression into the mold of a definite economic theory. Various ad hoc attempts to extricate a given economy from a slump received, for the first time, a set of official scriptures and a generation of economic planners was born and launched in the West, where until then (and to some people even now) economic planning had smacked of the communist experiments. The time soon came when an amazing discovery was made that even capitalist economy had always been "planned," and the state interference in economic life far from having had originated in 1933 (in the United States), or in 1945 (in Great Britain) is actually an ancient and honorable tradition. The discussion of economic planning has gone on ever since, with its opponents pointing out Soviet Russia as an example of what happens, ultimately and inevitably, as the result of the process, while the defenders of the new gospel always score a point by bringing up the specter of the Great Depression — a logical and unavoidable culmination of unplanned capitalism.

Beyond the sphere of irrelevant argument the social and political aspect of Keynes' theories has caught the imagination not only of social reformers, but also of politicians and civil servants. The logic of events in the thirties pointed clearly to a major breakdown of the traditional concepts of economics. The defenders of the old system could argue that the breakdown was due to causes having nothing to do with economic individualism, or that the haphazard measures taken to stem the depression were in reality responsible for its prolongation. But the neatness and logic of an argument cannot stem the tide of a social development, and the system which has broken down, even for reasons which may have nothing to do with its structure, is seldom allowed to remain unimpaired. In Great Britain the very cause which has contributed to the success of the Labour Party has also pushed on the acceptance of the new way of thinking about economic problems. Between the two world wars unemployment in Great Britain ranged from a minimum of just under ten per cent to a maximum over twenty-two and averaged 14.2 per cent of the working force.[18] This figure, and we may add to account for the families of the unemployed, or subtract a number for seasonal unemployed, stands for a large proportion of citizens for whom the mechanics of parliamentary government and the theories of democracies could have meant very little. A theory which promised to cure the scourge, without a major and time-consuming transformation of the whole social system, must have appeared more promising to the nation than the distant and doubtful benefits of socialism. The phenomenon of unemployment dominated the thinking of economists and politicians alike in the decade preceding the Second World War, and the attempts of believers in the old system to minimize or to dismiss its importance ran against the logic of the situation.[19] It is difficult to argue that any political system, and especially a democracy, can afford to have a considerable proportion of its citizens unemployed and supported by the state on a permanent

[18] Beveridge, *Full Employment in a Free Society*, p. 47.

[19] "Now if the system had another run such as it had in the sixty years preceding 1928 and really reached the $1300 per head of population, it is easy to see that all the desiderata that have so far been espoused by any social reformers—practically without exception, including even the greater part of the cranks—either would be fulfilled automatically, or could be fulfilled without a significant interference with the capitalist process. Ample provision for the unemployed in particular would then be not only tolerable, but a light burden. Irresponsibility in creating unemployment and in financing the support of unemployed might of course at any time create insoluble problems. But managed with ordinary prudence, an average annual expenditure of 16 billions on an average number of 16 million unemployed including dependents (10 per cent of the population) would not in itself be a serious matter with an available national income of 200 billion dollars (purchasing power of 1928) . . . I do not think unemployment is among those evils which, like poverty, capitalist evolution could eliminate of itself." Schumpeter, *Capitalism, Socialism, Democracy*, p. 69. Professor Schumpeter is using, of course, the example of the United States but his figures and meaning have a general application.

basis. The argument brought up by some classical economists, that unemployment is due to artificial rigidity in wage structure produced by the domination of unionism and the acceptance by the state of social welfare philosophies, possesses a small degree of relevance to present-day problems, for it is difficult to imagine today a democratic society without trade unions or a government which turns its back upon social problems.

The seed of the policies of the Labour Government of today lies in their acceptance of the idea of planning. Economic planning usually means a deliberate and conscious choice of economic priorities by a public authority.[20] It is thus but a more conscious and direct extension of what governments have always done, even in the days of economic individualism, by their fiscal policies, the character of their expenditures, and so forth. This time planning is done on a vastly increased and more direct scale with a social philosophy stated rather than inherent in the measures.

During the last war Sir William (now Lord) Beveridge, who had in the past, as an economist, drafted some of the most important measures of social legislation on the statute books in Great Britain, was charged by the Coalition Government with preparing an outline of social and economic policies to be followed when the war ended. The result was Beveridge's famous Report and his subsequent book on the same subject. Beveridge's proposals are clearly seen in the policies pursued by the Labour Government since 1945, and indeed one of the reasons for the defeat of the Conservatives in 1945 may have been the suspicion that they would not pursue, wholeheartedly, the measures to which they had given a somewhat grudging approval during the war.

The title of Beveridge's book, *Full Employment in a Free Society*, is very characteristic of his main emphasis. In the first place, it is an acknowledgment that there is little sense in economic security or prosperity if democratic institutions are not to be preserved and strengthened. An unfree society, like Soviet Russia, may have little trouble in achieving full employment but the means used for this purpose could not be tolerated in a democratic country.

Secondly, the book implies strongly that the main if not the

[20] B. Wootton, *Freedom Under Planning*, p. 6.

only problem confronting an industrial country like Great Britain is the prevention of unemployment. This is more than a treatise on economics or on some isolated social problem. The book exudes a whole social and political philosophy of its own, and it takes away little from Beveridge's own achievement to assert that he manages to say nothing very original, but that he combines and develops the social and economic ideas of a whole school. The book may be frowned upon by economists in the strict sense of the word, for it is really a throwback to the concept of political economy, a blend of economic and social considerations. The idea of almost unlimited possibilities for state direction of economic life is expressed by Beveridge in a language which is also distant from that of economic treatises:

All that can be done is to see that the pilot has necessary controls and an instrument board to tell him when and how to use the controls. It is necessary also that the pilot should always have the will to use the controls by which alone he can reach his destination.[21]

Full employment for Beveridge (its specific meaning: always more jobs offered at fair prices than there are temporarily unemployed men) requires definite powers at the disposal of the state to cut down chaotic conditions of the labor market. His recommendations look to (1) maintaining of total outlay adequate to provide full employment; (2) controlling location of industry; (3) securing organized mobility of labor.[22]

Total outlay means not only that the state should regulate the flow of investments, or that it should fill in the gap left by inadequate private investments. The state should also secure a steady and rising level of consumption. The optimistic assumption inherent in the plan is, again, that the state can do all these things largely as a matter of manipulation and that the organic resources of the society needed for a raised standard of living are always to be found somehow. Beveridge seems to ignore, too, the frequently made criticism that government spending discourages private investments, and the consequent purely economic problems of mixed economy.

[21] *Beveridge*, p. 38.
[22] *Ibid.*, p. 29.

The economic argument and the considerations of social welfare are blended together in Beveridge, some would say, to the disadvantage of the former. He has a somewhat lyrical approach to economics, typical of so many social planners.[23] On their social side Beveridge's proposals imply, of course, a continued high level of taxation in Great Britain. This in itself is a continuation of a long-existent trend, abhorrent as it would have been to old-school liberals. The modern democratic state looks with a disapproving eye at great inherited property, and modern statesmen no longer urge that money should be allowed to fructify in the taxpayer's pocket, as did Gladstone. Whether a mixed economy, which Beveridge prefers to a purely socialist one, can stand the strain of continued high taxation of private income is another question.

The helping hand of the community is to be extended in many ways. New improved schemes of national insurance are recommended. A national health service is to be set up bringing medical help within the reach of everybody. One of the most concrete proposals is the one for a national nutrition policy, to prevent the scandalous disparities in standards of nutrition which led to the paradoxical situation during the war when most Englishmen had a better diet from their reduced food stocks than they had had before.[24] Education is also to be extended and strengthened. The preoccupation with adult education so typical of a long line of British reformers is repeated in Beveridge.

The attack against unemployment is thus to be pursued on two fronts which are equally important. The net result of a successful campaign should be purely technological and seasonal unemployment never going above three per cent of the total working force (even taking into account the possibility of fluctuation in foreign trade).[25]

The maintenance of a total outlay sufficient to eliminate unemployment is the most important point of Beveridge's program. The other two main points deal even more directly with men, their choices and prejudices than does the control of investment and

[23] E.g., "The object of all human activity is not employment, but welfare, to raise the material standard of living and make opportunities for wider spiritual life." *Ibid.*, p. 147.

[24] *Ibid.*, p. 161.

[25] *Ibid.*, p. 128.

subsidizing of consumption. The problem of controlling the location of industries is a fairly uncontroversial one. It was recommended by the Barlow Commission, and it ties in with the proposal that land and town planning should be put on a rational and centrally controlled basis (the former always implies to a modern reformer the latter). The control of industrial and land development brings with it serious limitations upon the liberty of the citizens, and would have seemed, not so long ago, an intolerable imposition, but today there are few voices raised, even among the Conservatives, against these aspects of human engineering. The prayer that the state should mitigate the squalor and discomfort of urbanization has been uttered by almost every English social reformer.

But it is the problem of "organized mobility of labor" which introduces us to the most serious dilemma of planned society: the problem of incentives in a society where extreme poverty has been, on paper at any rate, eliminated; and the closely related problem of industrial discipline. What if the worker refuses to move to another location or another employment? Workers in the new utopia cannot be treated as a mere industrial army, segments of which are to be told from time to time to move on to another place or another industry or else! The question is treated very gingerly by Beveridge. All that he can bring himself to envisage in the way of sanctions is a system of withholding or minimizing unemployment benefits to a recalcitrant worker. Or as Mrs. Wootton puts it:

In effect the only way to combine universal freedom from want with the use of strictly economic sanction against excessive or deficient mobility is to widen the margin between the minimum subsistence in all cases, even of voluntary unemployment, and the normal insurance benefit payable as of right to the "genuinely" unemployed by pushing the latter generously upward.[26]

But the problem cannot be dismissed so lightly. Administratively the difference between "genuine" and "voluntary" unemployment is not easy to determine when one deals with a large number of cases. Under schemes of social welfare, the threat of

[26] B. Wootton, *Freedom Under Planning*, p. 100.

unemployment is removed as an incentive to harder work, that is, to higher productivity. What is to takes its place when the policy of the national minimum is combined with restrictive trade-union practices and the unwillingness to change the structure of wages in order to reward higher productivity? Beveridge writes hopefully that "The essence of civilization is that men should come to be led more and more by hope and ambition and example and less by fear." [27] But hope and ambition in material terms cannot be rewarded conspicuously by a society bent upon abolishing great disparities in wealth. The ideal of working for the community as a whole is certainly an important factor, and in times of national emergency and war the British worker has certainly responded to it. But to put this single motive as an everyday proposition and to expect that it will work miracles with productivity is to expect too much from human nature. Beveridge himself admits that statistics prove that disallowances of unemployment benefits (due to the refusal to work or to willful abandonment of a job) were twice as numerous in times of prosperity as in times of depression.[28] Right after the war the mineworkers' union refused, for a time, to admit foreign labor to the coalpits, when there was a severe labor shortage and a desperate need for more coal. The attitude may be ascribed to the self-protecting instinct of the worker, bred by the long years of exploitation and unemployment. It is doubtful, though, whether the absence of unrestrained capitalism or state ownership can by itself change these attitudes completely and it certainly cannot change them at all except after a number of years, during which the fate of national economy may lie in balance.

Similar problems are to be confronted by the welfare state in the related fields of wage fixing, labor disputes, and so forth. Barbara Wootton sees labor unions as being, due to their tradition, somewhat antisocial and sectional in their outlook, and she admits that the task of fitting them into economic planning is one of tremendous complexity.[29] Beveridge expresses hope that the right to strike, while not to be tampered with by the state, would become

[27] Beveridge, p. 198.
[28] *Ibid.*, p. 196.
[29] B. Wootton, p. 133.

eventually under the new conditions obsolete.[30] But one is reminded of the nineteenth-century liberals when they abolished the
legislation prohibiting strikes, on the ground that economic progress and human rationality would relegate labor disputes to the
realm of obsolete customs. Every reformer expects as the result
of his proposed measures an improvement of human nature to the
extent that, if it were possible, no reforms would be necessary in
the first place.

What does Beveridge's plan mean in terms of politics? The
author is emphatic that his plan does not involve commitment
either to socialism or to capitalism. The decision between the two
must come on the grounds of efficiency or social justice, but his
plan is compatible with either.[31] The assertion may be taken with
a grain of salt; Beveridge leans slightly but unmistakably towards
a pattern of moderate, democratic socialism. But there is nothing
inherently socialist in the plan, unless an extensive scheme of
social security and government controls is, as it should not be,
identified with socialism. Various industries, according to Beveridge, may or may not be socialized. What is much more important
is government supervision and direction of fiscal and industrial
policies. There are plausible grounds for claiming that the last-
mentioned postulate is in the long run destructive of what we
know as free enterprise and conducive to socialism, but then we
would have to admit that there are many socialists in Great Britain, not all of them in the Labour Party. We have an example
which may be instructive in that connection. In the early thirties
when Great Britain was shaking off the effects of depression,
Harold Macmillan, then a leader of the younger element in the
Conservative Party, came forth with proposals which in some respects anticipated Beveridge. His book starts with an outright condemnation of the "old" concept of capitalism.[32] It goes on to
propose a sort of New Deal for Great Britain, but in a more systematic and thorough way than the way in which the American

[30] Beveridge, p. 201.
[31] *Ibid.*, p. 252.
[32] "We must realize the essential contradictions of laissez-faire even while we
may appreciate the energy and drive of a rugged individualism." H. Macmillan,
Reconstruction: A Plea for a National Policy, p. 6.

experiment was conceived. Mr. Macmillan does not propose to abandon capitalism, but to strengthen it by bringing it up to date. His economic thinking is quite confused, but he goes far to prove that even on the Conservative side, even then, the idea of economic planning was not confused with socialism.

The key to Macmillan's plan is industrial self-government in major industries.[33] Every such industry is to have a council including the industrialists, representatives of labor, scientists, and technicians. All the industrial councils are to join in a central economic council to be linked firmly and unmistakably with the government. And the plan breathes some of the atmosphere of the NRA; the goal is an expanding economy with higher wages and more leisure. If private interests are to have a strong voice on the industrial councils, so are the trade unions.[34] One of the troubles of capitalism is diagnosed as the workers' feeling of being just cogs in the industrial machine. Hence the plan for an annual wage and for an extensive scheme of social services which, Macmillan hopes, will reintroduce the feeling of craftsmanship and permanence into labor, and will end the notion of the worker as a commodity.

In relation to the policies of the Conservative Party (then in power) at this period, Macmillan's book is an attempt to crystallize what might be called the spirit of reforming capitalism. There are hints in it of limiting production by intra-industry agreements, but the book faces boldly the prospect of economic planning even if the main burden of planning is to be done by the state rather than by the industrialists. The official policy at the time was that of economic orthodoxy and of trying to cope with the effects of depression by ad hoc policies.

Beveridge's plan, unlike Macmillan's, ties its proposals to a broad critique of the economic structure of capitalism. It goes halfway towards socialism. There is many a characteristic turn of phrase which indicates Beveridge's perhaps unconscious acceptance of the premises of socialism, if not of its conclusions. In speaking about the problem of freedom in the society which he recommends, the author subdivides the concept into a number of "liberties," and writes with not very good logic:

[33] *Ibid.*, p. 21.
[34] *Ibid.*, p. 113.

The lot of essential liberties given above does not include liberty of a private citizen to own means of production and to employ other citizens in operating at a wage . . . It is not an essential citizen liberty in Britain because it is not and never has been employed by more than a very small proportion of the British people.[35]

The statement is echoed by Mrs. Wootton.[36] While one may agree that the right to own the means of production is not an essential one, the argument used by Beveridge and Mrs. Wootton is un-convincing. The same "numerical" argument could be used to destroy the essential character of the right of private ownership of newspapers, the right to make political speeches, and so forth. In their thinking upon many related problems some of the leaders of the Labour Party have betrayed their willingness to follow the same criterion of distinguishing between "essential" and "unes-sential" liberties. The type of argument used by Beveridge reveals once more that he is writing more than just a treatise on some practical aspects of national economy; it reveals the roots of his social and political thinking. Twisted around it is easy to see that once we have condemned a "liberty" as "unessential," the temptation is very strong to declare the given class of rights as being antithetical to social justice and freedom. The next step is nationalizing industries for the sake of nationalization, as some have accused the Labour Government of doing.

Beveridge himself does not espouse the cause of indiscriminate nationalization, though his book leaves the door open to it. Himself a Liberal, Beveridge in his book formulated a practical program for the Labour Party which has carried it out since its victory in 1945. The provisions for social security, for stabilizing the price of necessaries, for an extensive health service—they have all been appropriated by the Labour Party, as has also been the broad definition of full employment which Beveridge adopted.[37] The Labour Party has found in the Beveridge Report a practical electoral platform. The report stirred the imagination of the country

[35] Beveridge, p. 23.
[36] B. Wootton, p. 122.
[37] "The difference between the definition of full employment in the Nuffield College statement, of slightly fewer vacant jobs than unemployed men, and that adopted here of more jobs than unemployed men is important from the social point of view. It affects the relation of the individual and his sense of values to the community." Beveridge, p. 131.

during the war, and though its principles were accepted by all the parties, the suspicion remained that the party of "vested interests" and of big business was not the one to carry it through. Even more effectively has the mentality behind the report expressed the assumptions and expectations of civil servants and ministers. Here was a reasonable program embodying everything that reasonable men could agree upon: capitalism still officially undisturbed, but also a great deal of collectivism, and the type of conclusions and objectives with which no sane man could quarrel. In contradistinction to some previous definitions of social planning, most of them emerging from socialists, Beveridge's plan contained no doctrinaire insistence upon definite political and structural changes. Its value as an electoral platform was obviously much greater than that of a declaration devoted to nationalization and to such stale political issues as the reform or abolition of the House of Lords.

There have been a few voices raised against the main assumptions of social planning. They are perhaps most characteristically expressed in Mr. Hayek's *Road to Serfdom*. The argument that social and economic planning is inherently wicked, destructive both of political freedom and of economic prosperity, is not likely, however, to carry much weight in this age. The logic of social events is sometimes different from that of pure economy, and even if the economic argument of Mr. Hayek (repeated more recently by Professor Jewkes[38]) were sound, there is no reversing of the tendency which has dominated political and social life in the West for some time.

On the other hand we have had enough experience with economic planning not to accept Beveridge's assumptions unquestioningly. There is undoubted idealism in Beveridge's objectives, to which no one can object. But that idealism also pervades his assumptions. If for a moment we could see his plan working smoothly, we would see the capitalist always ready to take small profit and to invest it where the community needs it; the worker invariably willing to accept state decision on his wages and the unions ready to forego restrictive practices; and the nations of the world coördinating their trade and fiscal policies. One might seriously ask whether a system of pure laissez faire might not also be

---

[38] *Ordeal by Planning* (London, 1948).

workable, if each of these assumptions were one-hundred-per-cent realistic?

Then, speaking more specifically about Great Britain, Beveridge glosses over the very serious problems connected with Britain's dependence upon international trade and with the certain changes which were sure to take place at the end of the war. Isn't the whole concept of a high standard of living for Great Britain dependent on her imperial and commercial position, and once this is undermined can the manipulation of the interest rate, the planning of consumption and production, overcome the basic deficiencies?

Those are grave questions which five years of strictly planned economy, very largely on the lines recommended by Beveridge, have not yet answered one way or another. To some extent Beveridge's plan is consonant with political democracy, as more drastic and doctrinaire planning on the one hand might not be, and the relative lack of planning expressed by a return to the nineteenth-century economic thinking, as Hayek would have it, certainly could not be. It is unfair to expect from a theoretical exposition of a social problem perfect adjustability to the actual conditions of life. The type of reform proposed by Beveridge is an advance upon the arid and doctrinaire political postulates many socialist reformers have advanced. The social implications of the plan are also in the great tradition which we have studied beginning with Green.

THE REFORM

It was an open question at the end of the First World War whether the Labour Party as a major political party would fit into the tradition of British parliamentary life. The aftermath of the war saw a gradual decline of the Liberal Party, and it was only natural that in the country with the highest proportion of industrial population in the world, the party representing the wishes and aspirations of the working class should assume a major political role. At the same time political life in Great Britain underwent an undoubted process of polarization. The party which, for all its links with the middle class, represented the interests of the trade union confronted the party standing for the aristocratic and imperial tradition, with its leadership drawn not only from the families which had ruled England for centuries but also from big business. The gap between the two parties may have seemed at some points during the period between the wars too great for an effective functioning of parliamentary government. There were periods of unusual strain as during the General Strike of 1926. In its two brief terms in office the Labour Party could not get on with the program of reform because, among other things, it did not possess a majority in the House of Commons and was consequently dependent upon the grudging support of the Liberals. It must have appeared to some leaders of the Labour Party that the parliamentary game was not worth playing from their point of view, that even a temporary victory at the polls would not be worth while since so many social forces were opposed to socialism, and that the enemy entrenched in the civil service would know how to frustrate a Labour electoral victory.

The feeling perhaps reached its height after 1931 when the Labour Party felt itself (with some justification) to have been cheated out of office and to have had its leaders kidnaped by the other side. For perspective on today it is useful to take a look at a Socialist League publication of 1933, *Problems of a Socialist Government*, and to see how some of today's leaders then envisaged these problems. Sir Stafford Cripps, then very much on the left of the Labour Party, wrote:

Continuity of policy — even in fundamentals — can find no place in a Socialist programme. It is this complete severance with all traditional theories of government, this determination to seize power from the ruling class and transfer it to the people as a whole, that differentiates the present political struggle from all those that have gone before.[39]

That the House of Lords would challenge socialist legislation and that the civil service would obstruct it was taken for granted. It was even envisaged that the Conservatives would refuse, when defeated during an election, to surrender their power.[40] The

---

[39] S. Cripps and others, *Problems of a Socialist Government*, p. 36.

[40] "If the Socialist came to the conclusion that there was any real danger of such a step being taken, it would probably be better and more conducive to the general peace and welfare of the country for the Socialist government to make itself temporarily into a dictatorship until the matter could again be put to test at the polls." Cripps, *ibid.*, p. 46.

transition to a socialist commonwealth was to take place without too much care for constitutional niceties. Once having obtained majority in the House of Commons the Socialist Party was to vote emergency powers to the government similar to the Defence of the Realm Acts passed during the war. From then on the state would, presumably, take over industries, issue regulations, and so forth, just as a matter of administrative procedure.[41] While Mr. Cole does not advocate outright expropriation he comes very close to it.[42]

The tone of this socialist symposium suggested radical hostility toward the conventions and traditions of British politics. Reading it, one could not have suspected that the writers represented one of the mildest and least doctrinaire socialist movements in Europe. Here, it seemed, was an unbridgeable gap between the two great parties, with ominous consequences for the future of parliamentary institutions and liberties in Great Britain.

What happened between 1933 and 1945 was not only the war, which saw the participation of the Labour Party in government and the decline of the dangerous feeling that the game of politics was fixed in favor of the party of the status quo, but also a revolution which took place in people's minds, and which left to the Labour Party, when it unexpectedly emerged victorious in 1945, the task of legalizing and putting into effect the conclusions that a great majority of Englishmen had arrived at before. It is very doubtful, had the Conservatives been victorious in 1945, that the general direction of reforms if not their actual shape would have been much different. The Conservatives never had the prejudice in favor of laissez faire which was characteristic of the Liberal Party in the nineteenth century. Insofar as their present social philosophy goes, they do not diverge too much from the position of Labour on social legislation, though opposing the further extension of the principle of nationalization of industries. On their part the Labour Party has moved along the road to

[41] G. D. H. Cole, *ibid.*, p. 155.

[42] "I therefore suggest that, where an industry or enterprise is taken over, the State, as part of the reorganization should be prepared to pay to its previous owners an allowance fixed, say for four or five years, at a proportion of the income actually received by those owners on the average of the previous years. Not the full income, be it observed, but a proportion, and not necessarily the same proportion in all schemes." Cole, *ibid.*, p. 164.

moderation. It has not abandoned its ultimate goals but it has adjusted itself to its responsibilities as a party in power, at least in the sense of moving slowly and recognizing the priority of the economic welfare of the country over its ideological postulates.

The last statement can, of course, be challenged. The Labour government has proceeded to nationalize the Bank of England and a whole line of major industries. It can be claimed that the argument for nationalization is a doctrinaire one and that in the present situation of Great Britain nationalization brings in an element of economic disruption which the country can ill afford. But the most important of the industries nationalized up to now — coal — has been in need of a drastic step for a long time. Had the Conservatives been in power, it is likely that the same step would have been undertaken under a different name. In the case of other industries (gas, electricity, transport, civil aviation, railways), there were considerations of efficiency or of the monopolistic character of the industries concerned which would have tempted even a mildly radical government to bring them under direct state control. The terms of compensation for the shareholders, while naturally criticized at times, do not even suggest anything approaching expropriation. The issue of nationalization of major industries does not represent a complete challenge to the concept of private property. It does confront the state with the ever increasing sphere of governmental activity and control. There must be serious repercussions in the fact that under a scheme of comprehensive nationalization a large part of the population would become employees of the state. The specter of "bureaucracy" is too readily raised by the opponents of any state interference in economic life. Nevertheless there are purely mechanical and quantitative factors making one wonder what the effects of the increased outgrowth of state machinery will be. The problem of the new role of the trade unions, now confronting the state instead of private employers, is one of many aspects of the overall dilemma. Yet it is fatuous to expect by raising artificial fears to deflect the course of the modern state from the direction it must take. A substantial degree of government supervision in the economic life of a nation is unavoidable today, and the quarrel can only be over the extent and details of state intervention rather than whether it should take place at all.

The bewildering mass of social legislation undertaken by the Labour government has been really "prepared for in the minds of all" as Sidney Webb urged about sixty years ago. It remains to be seen whether the overall concept of social democracy is a workable one, and how far life, and specifically the condition of Great Britain today, will affect the blue-print.

It is useful to take a look at some of the measures of social reform put in effect in England in past few years. Unlike the economic reform — nationalization — they have been effected with the approval of all major political parties. The National Health and Social Insurance Acts have aroused political debate only on the points of detail. The Conservatives have agreed to the principle involved, reluctantly perhaps but as irreversibly as in the nineteenth century they approved the principle of democratic franchise.

The Social Insurance Act[43] stems directly from the Beveridge Report. It concludes the trend in legislation which has been prominent in England ever since Lloyd George's budgets. The trend has proceeded from a modest system of industrial insurance and old-age pensions to a full-blown plan of extensive (in principle if not in amount) benefits to the whole community. The notion that dole and any form of state support for the individual is demoralizing had been the most characteristic mark of the utilitarian code of the nineteenth-century liberalism. It would shock the spirits of Bentham and even of John Stuart Mill to see the state making cash allowances for every child but the first of every family. Beneath the measure a shocked Malthusian would find not "subsidization of consumption," which was the reason given by Beveridge for his proposal, but a new and vastly different social philosophy which holds that the state owes a minimum of maintenance to every member of the community. Even Green and Bosanquet, for they believed in the Victorian slogan of self-reliance, would look skeptically at the state guaranteeing a retirement pension for men and women after they reach, respectively, the ages of sixty-five and sixty. The vast system of social benefits extends to the rich (if they are still left after years of almost confiscatory taxation of high incomes) and the poor alike. There is very

---

[43] See *National Insurance Act, 1946*, H.M. Stationery Office.

little socialism, properly understood, in such measures, but a great deal of a philosophy different from both socialism and original liberalism. The state takes on the task of supporting, in principle, each of its citizens. In return it places certain effective limits on his pursuit of material self-improvement. The incentive to work can no longer be the expectation of making a great fortune, or even of blazing new roads in industry and other economic pursuits. The new social policy must assume a highly developed sense of social solidarity and discipline. It must also assume that a pressure of external events which would put a curb on economic expansion would not bring the whole social structure tottering down. Economic and social equality presented in a static form holds very little attraction for most people, and implicit in the new program, along with a great deal of socialist thinking (in a not too literal sense), is the faith that the new social system will prove more efficient economically than the old one. If that assumption is disproved one may expect not a return to economic liberalism, for the new orientations and aspirations are too deeply ingrained in people, but a new and basic challenge to the political system; because when the possibilities of democratic reforms are exhausted, the remaining dissatisfaction can still be channeled against democracy itself.

The very height of the conception of the welfare state is reached in the ideas embodied in the National Health Act.[44] The principle contained is that of universal "free" (that is, state supported) medical help and services. Again the main principles of the act had been conceived under the Coalition Government and it fell to the Labour Party to embody only a few more drastic provisions dealing with the administration of health services and with doctors' compensation. Though doctors can still stay out of the National Health Service and patients if they so desire can still obtain and pay for medical help, the long-run effect of the new system must result in the transformation of the medical profession and of health services into another branch of state services. All the assurances and concessions given by the government to the medical profession cannot alter the simple logic of the situation. The long-run success or failure of the new plan will provide

[44] See *National Health Act, 1946,* H.M. Stationery Office.

the most significant criterion of the applicability of the welfare state to a democratic society. The working of the new health plan bears upon the most crucial assumptions of the "planners": the willingness of the expert to work under conditions that assure him of a modicum of economic security, but deprive him, at least psychologically, of a certain independence, and which put a limit upon his expectations, if not the actual reality of material success; and the ability of the people to show rationality and restraint under a plan which offers great opportunities for individual abuses of the right of free medical services, and which, if abused on a large scale, might break down administratively and financially. The theories and hopes embodied in the National Health Act cannot be tested on the basis of a few years' experience. The judgment requires the trial run of something approaching a generation, but at the same time the act is a more thorough approach to the idea of the welfare state than could be contained in nationalizing all the major industries of a country.

The Education Act of 1944 belongs to the sum of social reforms which are transforming Great Britain today. The fact that the act was passed under the Coalition Government and that it was officially sponsored by one of the leading Conservatives, the then Minister of Education, Mr. Butler, serves to emphasize the point that there is no exclusive party label about the general direction of social reform in Great Britain. The act itself deals ostensibly with one of the most uncontroversial aspects (at least in England) of state activity. In its broad conception and outlook the new program for education is highly characteristic.[45] It conceives education to be a very broad area of social activity, rather than a process of selective training. Education is to be compulsory between the ages of five and fifteen, the latter limit to be raised ultimately to sixteen. (The Labour Government raised the terminal age to fifteen despite the current manpower shortage.) No fees are to be charged for attending the schools maintained by local education authorities and supervised by the Ministry of Education. The schools become, even more so than they were in the past, veritable social centers. They are to provide medical services to the students and provide the indigent ones with clothing. The school is to take

[45] *The Education Act of 1944*, H.M. Stationery Office.

notice of its pupils' employment, and to take appropriate steps if the work is in any way injurious to the children.

There was a time when democratic theories put almost unlimited trust in the possibilities of nation-wide education. It has been recognized on the basis of experience that the mere diffusion of literacy and knowledge does not in itself work miracles with human nature, and it certainly does not in itself assure a working democracy. There is much to be done, however, in extending universal education beyond the rudimentary level, which is hardly adequate in equipping a man for living and for citizenship in a modern society. The Education Act looks eventually to an extension of educational opportunities for everybody beyond the age of childhood. There is a provision in it for the establishment of part-time education for people between the ages of fifteen and eighteen. This is found in the provision for county colleges which are to be

centres approved by the Minister for providing for young persons who are not in full time attendance at any school or other educational institution such further education, including physical, practical, and vocational training as will enable them to develop their various aptitudes and capacities and will prepare them for the responsibilities of citizenship.[46]

When this part of the act is put into effect young people who are unable to go to a university or an advanced school will attend county colleges for three years, spending there one day a week or its equivalent throughout the year. Schooling on a compulsory basis is to continue until adult education, on a voluntary basis, can take over.

An interesting sidelight on the act is that it continues the previously developed method of combining the immediate supervision of the schools by the local authorities with the overall supervisory powers of the minister. Once the public authority acquires control over a segment of social life, be it in industry or in education, the problem immediately arises to what degree centralization is desirable or possible. In practice, if not in theory, the nationalized industries have been subjected to a high degree of centralization, but in education there are all sorts of valid reasons for allow-

[46] *Ibid.*, p. 34.

ing as much local autonomy as possible, and this seems to be the intent of the act.

The philosophy behind the Education Act is clearly that of extending as much free education to the masses as the country can afford. It fits in with the concept of democracy to diminish and ultimately, perhaps, to remove the sharp distinction that has existed in Great Britain between persons educated in publicly supported schools and those who went through private schools. A man as moderately conservative as Dicey saw in the Education Act of 1870 the beginning of the collectivist era in England.[47] The present plan for education in a sense completes the movement. At the same time the democratic objectives of the act are already being accomplished by other social forces than education, and by itself, imposing as it is in its concept, the Education Act is likely to have less significance than it would have had, had a more far-sighted country adopted it thirty or forty years ago.

The trend indicated in the social measures described above is an irresistible tendency of the modern state to advance along the road of greater social equality. Whatever private interests or biases may stand in the way of a comprehensive plan of social insurance, of universal education, of greater medical facilities for all, they are not allowed to express a vocal protest against *the principle* of such measures, any more than opposition to the principle of progressive taxation could be tolerated by a party with serious political ambitions. The democratic state is seized with the dynamism of the egalitarian drive, and the very fact that true conservatism can no longer be openly acknowledged makes political issues lose their clarity and jeopardizes the hope that the extension of democracy will follow the progress of social equality. In other words decisions of a democratic electorate must increasingly depend on the judgment of the performance of a given party in power and the expectation of its future performance rather than on its choice between two sets of principles. That in itself is nothing new insofar as the practice of politics goes. John Stuart Mill foresaw clearly the difficulty of a politician trying to preserve his principles against the tide of public opinion. But there is a danger point where the repudiation of clearly obsolete social and political

[47] See Chapter II, n. 42, above.

ideas passes into an insincere and unconvinced acceptance of popularity-seeking programs and slogans. The game of politics is then deprived of whatever rational examination of social issues it may possess. Political parties become driven purely by the logic of power seeking, and crucial decisions are in effect removed from the hands of the people.

The issue of nationalization offers an example of a political party being caught and propelled by its own ideological assumptions, and in the face of serious apprehensions of its leaders. Even before radical economists "showed" that control of major industries should be vested in the state for purely economic reasons, the Labour Party had believed that as a matter of social justice management of great industries should not be subject to private interests. Herbert Morrison, one of the architects of the victory in 1945, who took a leading part in formulating the program of the party, had written words characteristic of the socialist approach to the problem:

But I am all for speed. The vision of one Minister alone socialising two big industries in one year pleases me enormously . . . Socialism for me is a policy for today and not for some indefinite day after tomorrow . . . The function of Labour Governments in the future will rather be to secure the socialisation of industry after industry under a management which can broadly be relied upon to go on with its work. And having done one good deed the Minister can let the people put in charge carry on with the work thus done whilst he immediately sets about the other good deeds of socialization which await his attention.[48]

The rationale of nationalization was never adequately discussed except for emphasis on the general sinfulness of an important industry remaining under private power. There have been attempts to link criteria for nationalization with the monopolistic character of the given industry, its standard of efficiency, and so forth. But the main consideration was the fact that the demand for nationalization became a matter of faith with the Labour Party. The argument about the danger of an important part of the national economy remaining subject to private whims and interests lost much of its significance during the war when the state could control and direct industries without actually own-

[48] Herbert Morrison, *Socialisation and Transport*, p. 140.

ing them. It was obvious that certain industries had to be nationalized (for example, coal), if for nothing else than for purely psychological reasons. But the wholesale process of nationalization which had been actually forced upon the party's leaders before the 1945 elections, was to call the attention of the government from much more urgent tasks and was to strain the resources of state machinery. The proposition that the worker works harder, in peacetime, in a nationalized enterprise than he does in a private one, assumes a great degree of metaphysical skill and perhaps an excessive class feeling in an average person. The arguments of the believers in private enterprise about the inhumanness and inefficiency of bureaucracy can be equally well applied to large private monopolies. But the fact remains that state direction of great industrial enterprises is something which has to be worked out and tested under practical circumstances, and the haste with which the Labour Government has performed its experiment has jeopardized its overall program.

The basic fact about the program of reform which Great Britain has been going through in last few years is the human response to the changes in social structure. The conservative has claimed all along that increased security for the average individual and the heightened pace of state direction of all aspects of economic activity will slowly but surely enervate a society. The reformer has prophesied new vistas of creative effort and new fields of activity, once unemployment is banished and the helpful hand of the state has provided a modicum of economic security. Both must find in the present stage of the British experiment a confirmation of their fears and hopes. It is easy to condemn all such considerations as irrelevant and to point out the changes in Great Britain's external position and in the world situation as being mainly responsible for the particular situation Great Britain is in today. Social reforms do not succeed or fail because of the logic of the argument that can be advanced concerning the conditions under which they have to operate. What affects their success is their overall adequacy no matter how unfortunate or fortunate those conditions may chance to be. From this point of view it is difficult to call the socialist experiment, even today when the whole economy of the country is in mortal danger, anything less than a qualified success. Particular forms of industrial organization, of work incentives, and of social services can be changed or discarded. What cannot be changed or undone is the example of political democracy reaching into the sphere of social implementation and attempting a major reconstruction of society towards the ideal of social equality, something enemies of democracy have said could never be done by a "capitalist" state. The British experiment is therefore the vindication of the concept of the democratic state and its power of adaptability to changing social and economic circumstances. Its success or failure can affect the future of socialism, but it cannot destroy the visible proof of the reality of the democratic process.

And, in a different sense, it can be argued that the future of British socialism as distinct from the future of a political party is tied up with the future of democratic institutions. The concept of the welfare state has become part of the mold of democratic ideas and can no longer be detached without disfiguring British democracy. No change in the political scene can erase the major reforms from the statute book nor can it affect the notion that those reforms are an irreplaceable feature of a free society.

In that sense British socialism is a phenomenon at once wider and more significant than the ideologies of various socialist movements in Great Britain. It represents a definite stage in the development of political democracy, a stage prepared and analyzed by the idealism of philosophers and economists of whom many were nonsocialist or antisocialist in their beliefs.

Bibliography

Aristotelian Society Supplementary Volume VIII, *Mind, Matter, and Purpose*. London, 1928.

Barker, Ernest, *Political Thought in England, 1848–1914*. London, 1915.

——— *The Citizen's Choice*. Cambridge, 1937.

——— *Reflections on Government*. Oxford, 1942.

Barnard, Chester I., *The Functions of the Executive*. Cambridge, Massachusetts, 1945.

Beer, Max, *A History of British Socialism*. 2 vols. London, 1923.

Bentley, Arthur F., *The Process of Government*. Chicago, 1908.

Beveridge, William H., *Full Employment in a Free Society*. New York, 1945.

Bosanquet, Bernard, *Essays and Addresses*. London, 1891.

——— *Knowledge and Reality*. London, 1892.

——— *The Philosophical Theory of the State*. London, 1910.

——— *Truth and Coherence*. Glasgow, 1911.

——— *The Principle of Individuality and Value*. London, 1912.

——— *Social and International Ideals*. London, 1917.

——— *Implications and Linear Interference*. London, 1920.

——— *Science and Philosophy, and Other Essays*. London, 1927.

Bosanquet, Bernard, and others, *Philanthropy and Social Progress*. New York, 1893.

——— *Aspects of the Social Problem*. London, 1895.

Bradley, F. H., *Ethical Studies*. Oxford, 1927.

Brinton, Crane, *English Political Thought in the Nineteenth Century*. London, 1933.

Burnham, James, *The Machiavellians*. New York, 1943.

Caird, Edward, *Hegel*. Edinburgh, 1883.

——— *The Critical Philosophy of Immanuel Kant*. Glasgow, 1889.

Chin, Yueh Lin, *The Political Philosophy of Thomas Hill Green.* New York, 1920.

Cole, G. D. H., *Social Theory.* London, 1920.

—— *Guild Socialism Restated.* London, 1920.

—— *The World of Labour.* London, 1920.

—— *Economic Planning.* New York, 1935.

—— *The Fabian Society, Past and Present.* London, 1942.

Cole, G. D. H., and Raymond Postgate, *The British Common People, 1746–1938.* New York, 1939.

Cole, G. D. H., and others, *A Plan for Britain.* London, 1938.

Cole, Margaret, *Beatrice Webb.* New York, 1946.

Cripps, Sir Stafford, and others, *Problems of a Socialist Government.* London, 1933.

Dalton, Hugh, *Some Aspects of the Inequality of Incomes in Modern Communities.* London, 1920.

—— *Practical Socialism for Britain.* London, 1935.

Dewey, John, *German Philosophy and Politics.* New York, 1915.

Dickinson, G. Lowes, *A Modern Symposium.* New York, 1906.

—— *Justice and Liberty.* New York, 1909.

—— *The Choice Before Us.* London, 1917.

Dickinson, G. Lowes, and others, *Towards a Lasting Settlement.* London, 1916.

Durbin, E. F. M., *The Politics of Democratic Socialism.* London, 1940.

Elliott, W. Y., *Pragmatic Revolt in Politics.* New York, 1928.

Fabian Essays in Socialism. London, 1931.

Fairbrother, W. H., *The Philosophy of T. H. Green.* London, 1900.

Figgis, John Neville, *Churches in the Modern State.* London, 1913.

Fisher, Herbert, *The Commonweal.* Oxford, 1924.

Follett, M. P., *The New State.* New York, 1926.

Gordon, Lincoln, *The Public Corporation in Great Britain.* London, 1938.

Green, T. H., *Lectures on the Principles of Political Obligation.* London, 1895.

—— *Works.* R. L. Nettleship, ed. London, 1900.

—— *Prologomena to Ethics.* Oxford, 1929.

Hegel, *Lectures on the Philosophy of History.* J. Sibree, tr. London, 1894.

—— *Philosophy of Right.* S. W. Dyde, tr. London, 1896.

—— *The Phenomenology of Mind.* J. B. Baillie, tr. London, 1910.

Hobhouse, L. T., *Democracy and Reaction.* New York, 1905.

—— *The World in Conflict.* London, 1915.

—— *Questions of War and Peace*. London, 1916.

—— *The Metaphysical Theory of the State*. London, 1918.

—— *Social Evolution and Political Theory*. New York, 1922.

—— *The Mind in Evolution*. London, 1926.

Hobson, J. A., *The Crisis of Liberalism: New Issues of Democracy*. London, 1909.

—— *Confessions of an Economic Heretic*. London, 1938.

—— *Imperialism: A Study*. London, 1938.

—— *Democracy and a Changing Civilization*. London, 1939.

Hobson, S. G., *National Guilds and the State*. New York, 1920.

Hook, Sidney, *From Hegel to Marx*. London, 1936.

Hudson, Jay William, *Why Democracy*. New York, 1936.

Kant, Immanuel, *Critique of Pure Reason*. T. Max Muller, tr. London, 1929.

Keynes, J. M., *The Economic Consequences of the Peace*. New York, 1920.

—— *The General Theory of Employment, Interest, and Money*. New York, 1936.

Laski, Harold, *Authority in the Modern State*. New Haven, 1919.

—— *Faith, Reason, and Civilization*. New York, 1944.

Let Us Face the Future. Electoral Declaration of the Labour Party. New York, 1945.

Lindsay, A. D., *The Philosophy of Immanuel Kant*. London, 1914.

—— *The Essentials of Democracy*. Philadelphia, 1929.

—— *The Churches and Democracy*. London, 1934.

—— *Karl Marx's Capital, An Introductory Essay*. London, 1935.

—— *Toleration and Democracy*. London, 1942.

—— *The Modern Democratic State*. London, 1943.

Lynd, Helen Merrell, *England in the Eighteen Eighties*. London, 1945.

MacIver, R. M., *Community*. New York, 1928.

—— *Society*. New York, 1937.

Macmillan, Harold, *Reconstruction: A Plea for National Policy*. London, 1934.

—— *The Middle Way*. London, 1938.

Marcuse, Herbert, *Reason and Revolution: Hegel and the Rise of Social Theory*. London, 1941.

Morrison, Herbert, *Socialisation and Transport*. London, 1933.

—— *Prospects and Policies*. New York, 1944.

Muirhead, J. H., *The Service of the State: Four Lectures on the Political Teaching of T. H. Green*. London, 1908.

—— *Bernard Bosanquet and His Friends*. London, 1935.

Nettleship, Richard Lewis, *Memoir of T. H. Green*. London, 1902.

Niebuhr, Reinhold, *The Nature and Destiny of Man*. Vol. II, *Human Destiny*. New York, 1943.

Orage, A. R., *National Guilds*. London, 1914.

Pease, Edward R., *The History of the Fabian Society*. London, 1925.

Penty, Arthur J., *The Restoration of the Guild System*. London, 1906.

—— *Old Worlds for New*. London, 1918.

—— *Guilds and The Social Crisis*. London, 1919.

—— *Guilds, Trade and Agriculture*. London, 1921.

Pfannenstill, Bertil, *Bernard Bosanquet's Philosophy of the State*. Lund, 1936.

Pipkin, Charles W., *The Idea of Social Justice*. New York, 1927.

Ritchie, David G., *Natural Rights*. London, 1895.

Rockow, Lewis, *Contemporary Political Thought in England*. London, 1925.

Royce, Josiah, *The World and the Individual*. New York, 1900.

Schumpeter, Joseph, *Capitalism, Socialism, Democracy*. New York, 1942.

Sidgwick, Henry, *Lectures on the Ethics of T. H. Green, Mr. Herbert Spencer, and J. Martineau*. London, 1902.

Stace, W. T., *The Philosophy of Hegel*. London, 1929.

—— *The Destiny of the Western Man*. New York, 1942.

Tawney, R. H., *The Acquisitive Society*. New York, 1920.

—— *Equality*. London, 1931.

Wallas, Graham, *Human Nature in Politics*. London, 1914.

—— *The Great Society*. New York, 1914.

Webb, S. and B., *A Constitution for the Socialist Commonwealth of Great Britain*. London, 1920.

Wootton, Barbara, *Freedom Under Planning*. Durham, N. C., 1945.

Index